GUITAR
PLAY-ALONG

AUDIO
ACCESS
INCLUDED

KENNY WAYNE SHEPHERD

To access audio visit:
www.halleonard.com/mylibrary

Enter Code
8369-1296-7859-6838

Cover photo © JeromeBrunet.com

ISBN 978-1-4950-0249-6

HAL•LEONARD®
CORPORATION

7777 W. BLUEMOUND RD. P.O. BOX 13819 MILWAUKEE, WI 53213

Visit Hal Leonard Online at
www.halleonard.com

CONTENTS

GUITAR NOTATION LEGEND

THE MUSICAL STAFF shows pitches and rhythms and is divided by bar lines into measures. Pitches are named after the first seven letters of the alphabet.

TABLATURE graphically represents the guitar fingerboard. Each horizontal line represents a string, and each number represents a fret.

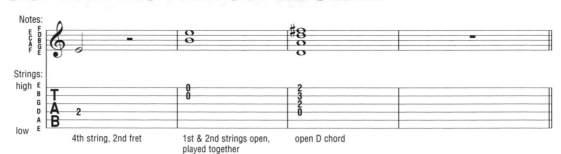

4th string, 2nd fret

1st & 2nd strings open, played together

open D chord

HALF-STEP BEND: Strike the note and bend up 1/2 step.

WHOLE-STEP BEND: Strike the note and bend up one step.

GRACE NOTE BEND: Strike the note and immediately bend up as indicated.

SLIGHT (MICROTONE) BEND: Strike the note and bend up 1/4 step.

BEND AND RELEASE: Strike the note and bend up as indicated, then release back to the original note. Only the first note is struck.

PRE-BEND: Bend the note as indicated, then strike it.

VIBRATO: The string is vibrated by rapidly bending and releasing the note with the fretting hand.

PALM MUTING: The note is partially muted by the pick hand lightly touching the string(s) just before the bridge.

HAMMER-ON: Strike the first (lower) note with one finger, then sound the higher note (on the same string) with another finger by fretting it without picking.

PULL-OFF: Place both fingers on the notes to be sounded. Strike the first note and without picking, pull the finger off to sound the second (lower) note.

LEGATO SLIDE: Strike the first note and then slide the same fret-hand finger up or down to the second note. The second note is not struck.

SHIFT SLIDE: Same as legato slide, except the second note is struck.

TRILL: Very rapidly alternate between the notes indicated by continuously hammering on and pulling off.

TAPPING: Hammer ("tap") the fret indicated with the pick-hand index or middle finger and pull off to the note fretted by the fret hand.

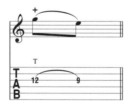

NATURAL HARMONIC: Strike the note while the fret-hand lightly touches the string directly over the fret indicated.

PINCH HARMONIC: The note is fretted normally and a harmonic is produced by adding the edge of the thumb or the tip of the index finger of the pick hand to the normal pick attack.

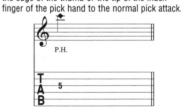

TREMOLO PICKING: The note is picked as rapidly and continuously as possible.

VIBRATO BAR DIVE AND RETURN: The pitch of the note or chord is dropped a specified number of steps (in rhythm), then returned to the original pitch.

VIBRATO BAR SCOOP: Depress the bar just before striking the note, then quickly release the bar.

VIBRATO BAR DIP: Strike the note and then immediately drop a specified number of steps, then release back to the original pitch.

Additional Musical Definitions

 (accent)   • Accentuate note (play it louder).

 (staccato)   • Play the note short.

D.S. al Coda   • Go back to the sign (%), then play until the measure marked "**To Coda**," then skip to the section labelled "**Coda**."

D.C. al Fine   • Go back to the beginning of the song and play until the measure marked "**Fine**" (end).

Fill   • Label used to identify a brief melodic figure which is to be inserted into the arrangement.

N.C.   • Harmony is implied.

• Repeat measures between signs.

• When a repeated section has different endings, play the first ending only the first time and the second ending only the second time.

Blue on Black

Words and Music by Tia Sillers, Mark Selby and Kenny Wayne Shepherd

Drop D tuning:
(low to high) D-A-D-G-B-E

Intro

Moderately slow ♩ = 78

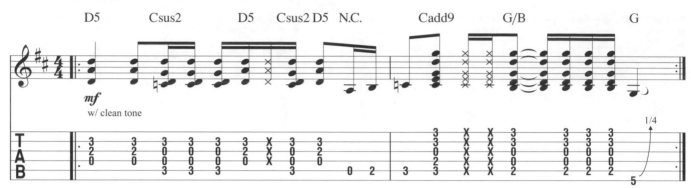

Verse

2nd time, substitue Fill 1

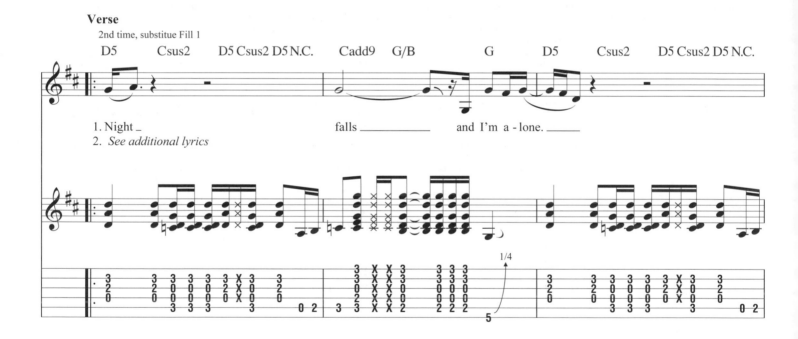

1. Night _ falls _____ and I'm a - lone. _____
2. *See additional lyrics*

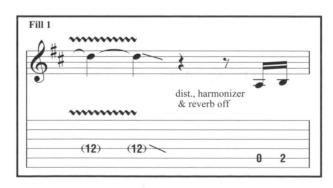

Fill 1

dist., harmonizer & reverb off

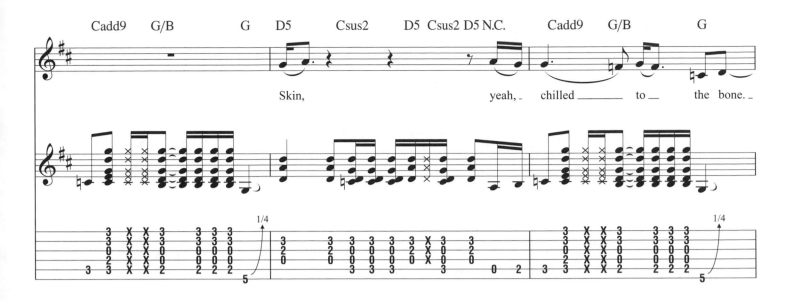

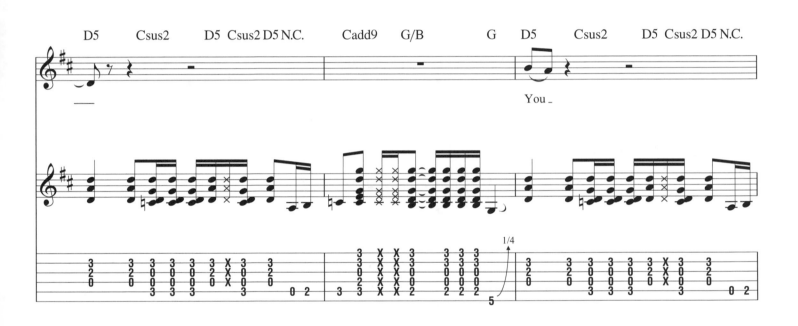

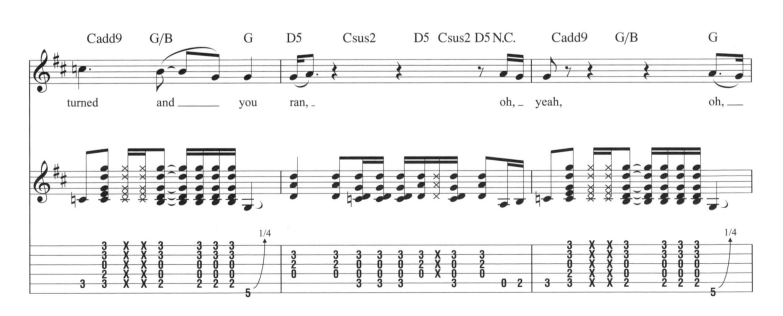

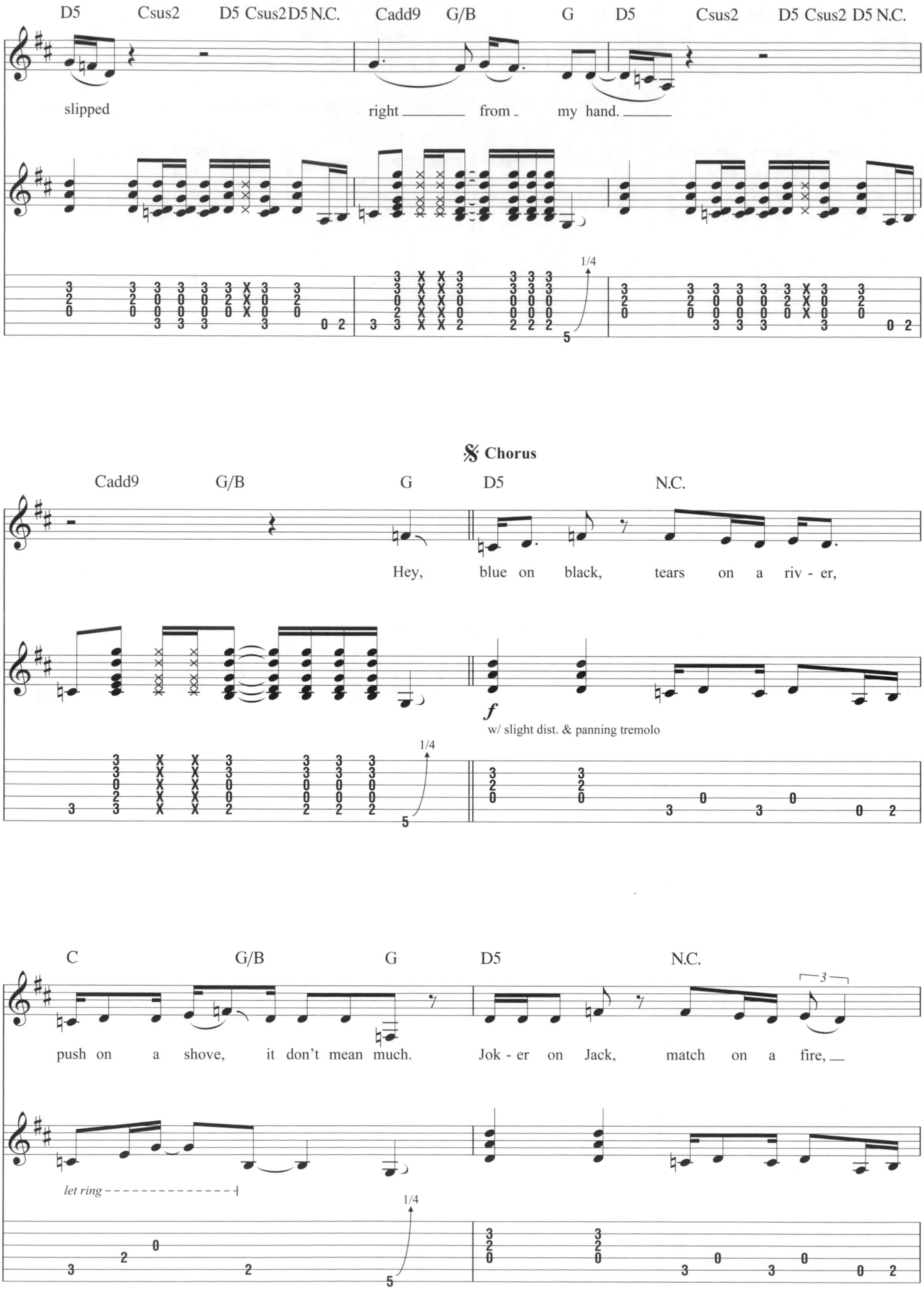
D5 Csus2 D5 Csus2 D5 N.C. Cadd9 G/B G D5 Csus2 D5 Csus2 D5 N.C.
slipped right from my hand.
1/4
Chorus
Cadd9 G/B G D5 N.C.
Hey, blue on black, tears on a riv - er,
f
w/ slight dist. & panning tremolo
1/4
C G/B G D5 N.C.
push on a shove, it don't mean much. Jok - er on Jack, match on a fire,
let ring
1/4

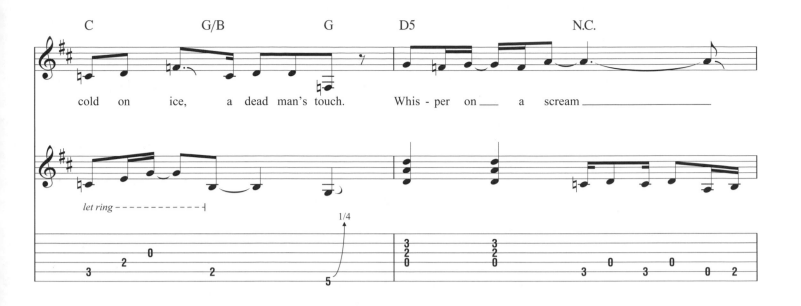

cold on ice, a dead man's touch. Whis-per on ___ a scream _____

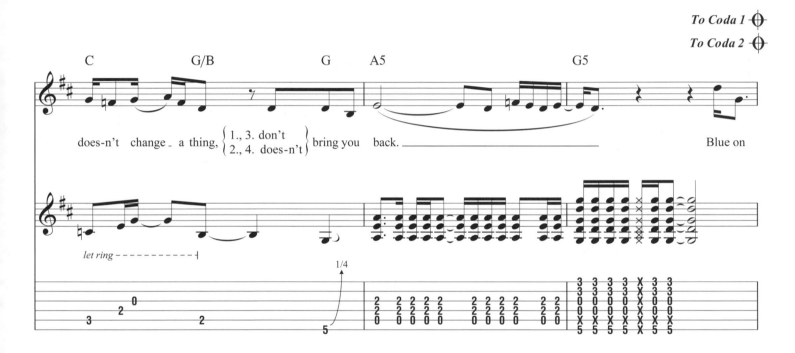

doesn't change ___ a thing, {1., 3. don't / 2., 4. does-n't} bring you back. _____ Blue on

To Coda 1 ⊕
To Coda 2 ⊕

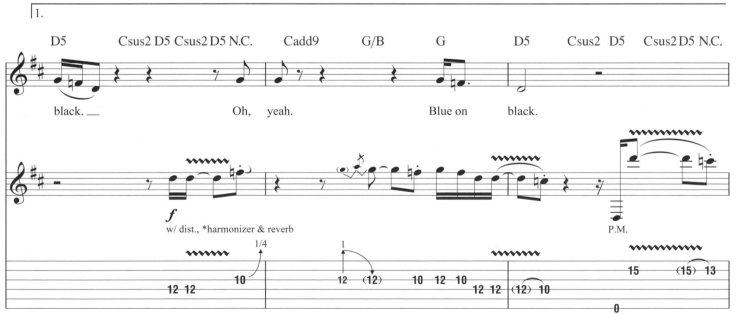

black. ___ Oh, yeah. Blue on black.

*Set to harmonize one octave above.

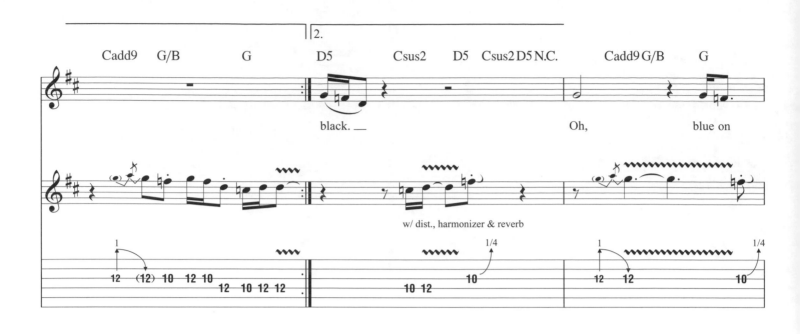

black. ___   Oh,   blue on

w/ dist., harmonizer & reverb

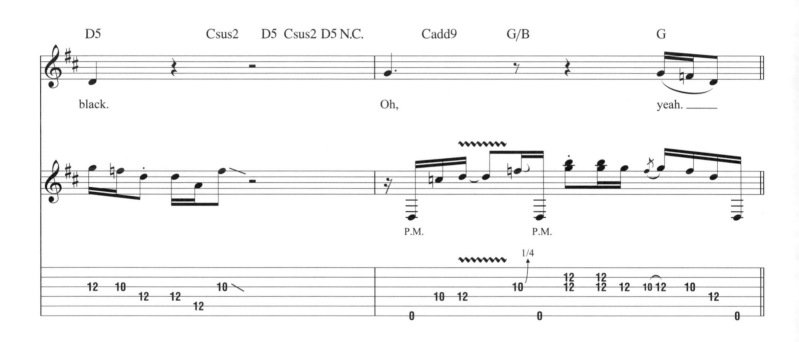

black.   Oh,   yeah. ___

Guitar Solo

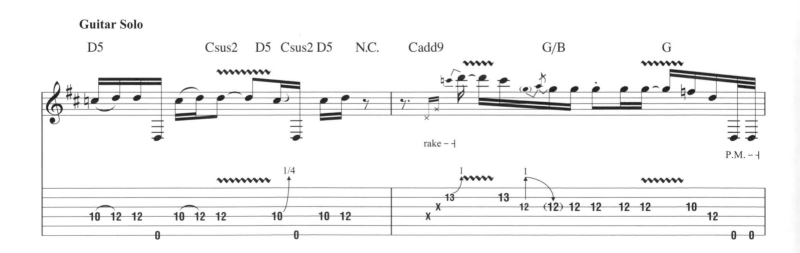

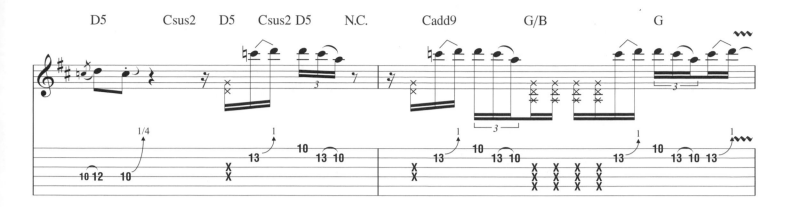

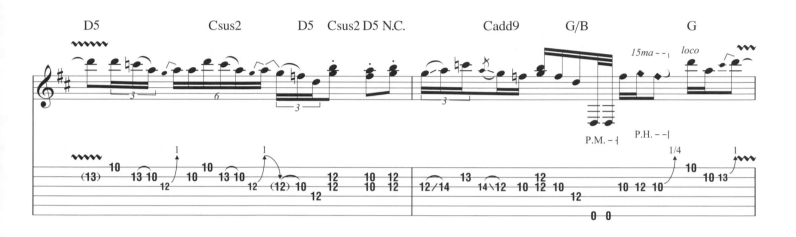

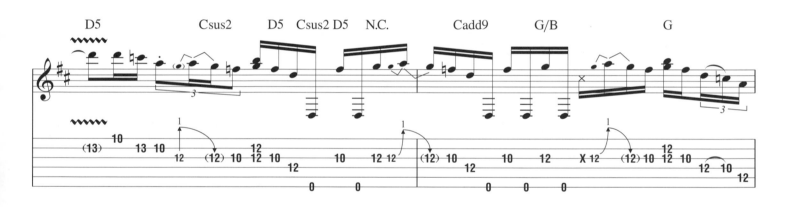

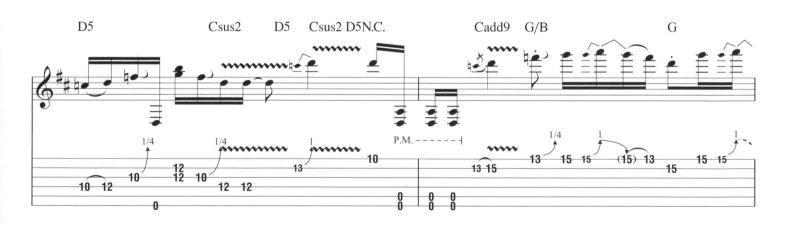

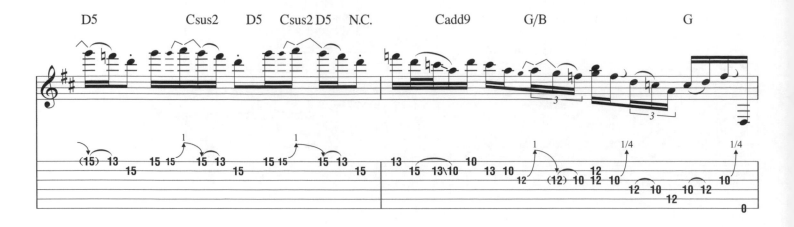

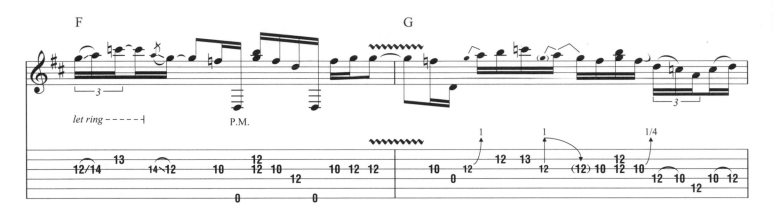

D.S. al Coda 1

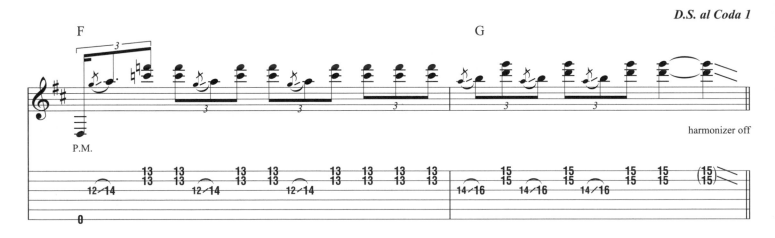

Coda 1

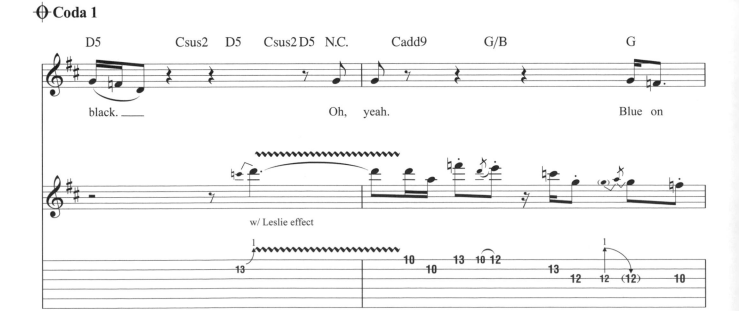

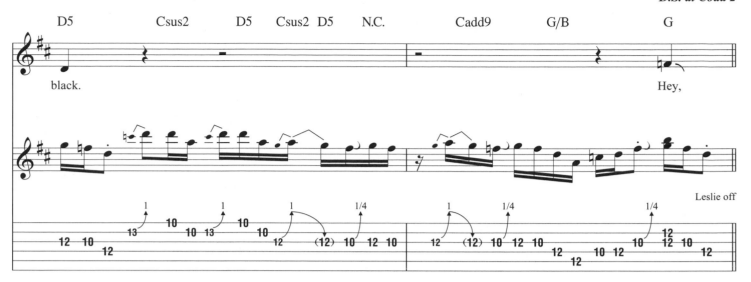

Coda 2

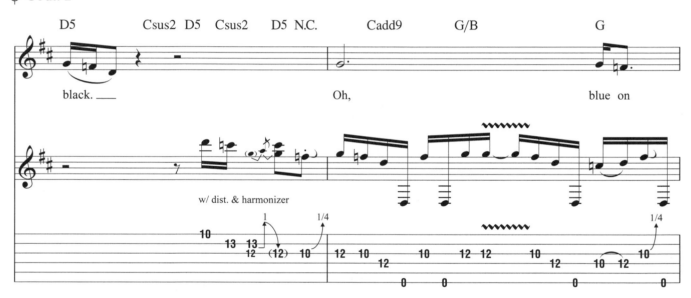

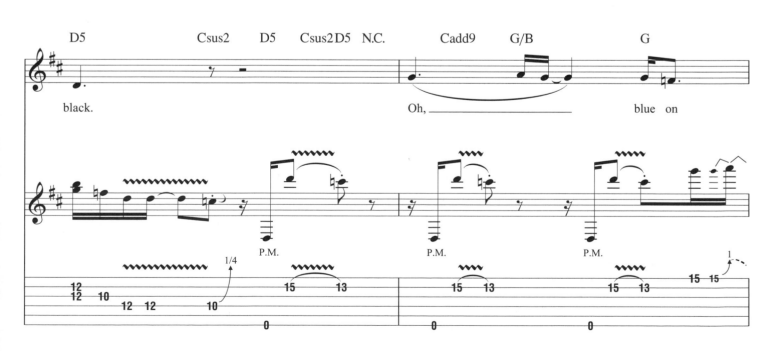

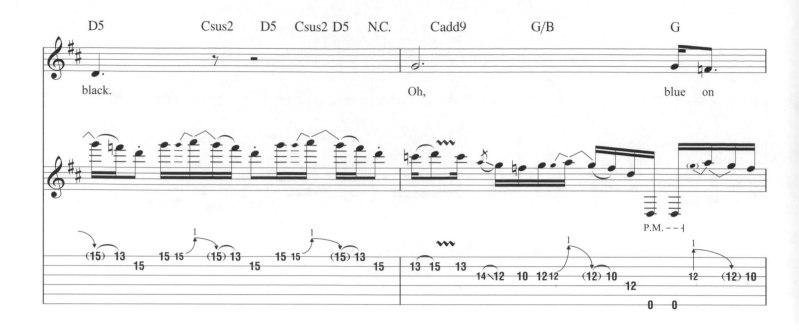

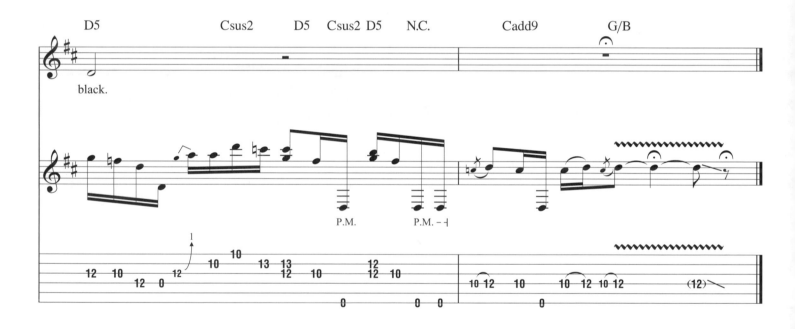

Additional Lyrics

2. Blind, oh, and now I see
   Truth, lies and in between.
   Wrong can't be undone.
   Oh, slipped from the tip of your tongue.

Born With a Broken Heart

Words and Music by Danny Tate and Kenny Wayne Shepherd

Tune down 1/2 step:
(low to high) Eb-Ab-Db-Gb-Bb-Eb

Intro
Moderate Blues ♩. = 111

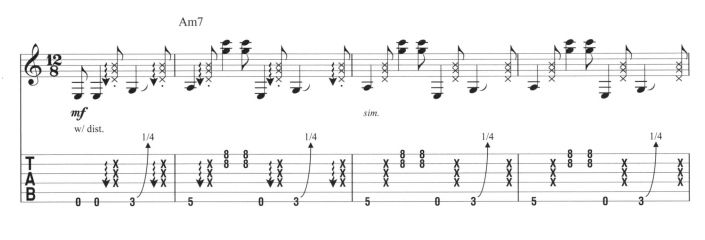

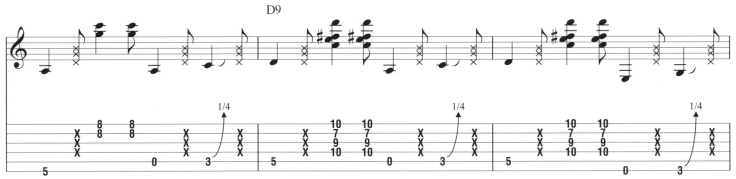

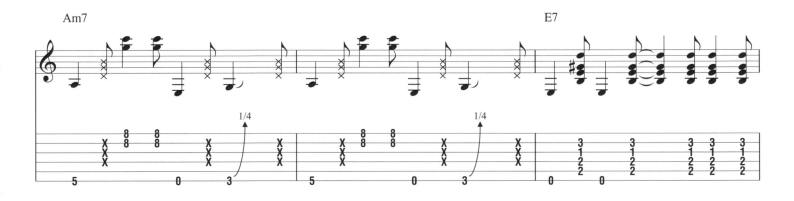

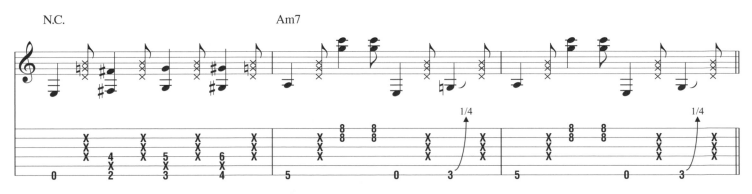

Coda 1

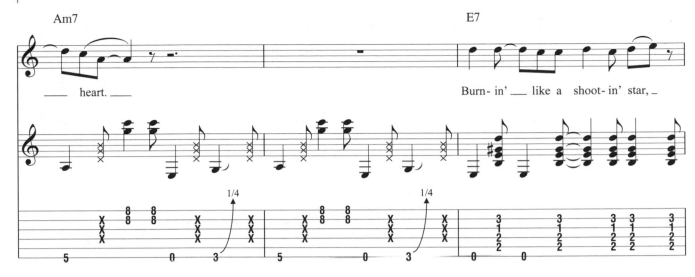

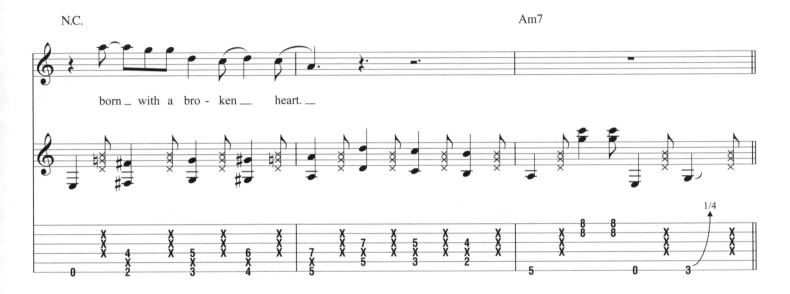

Guitar Solo

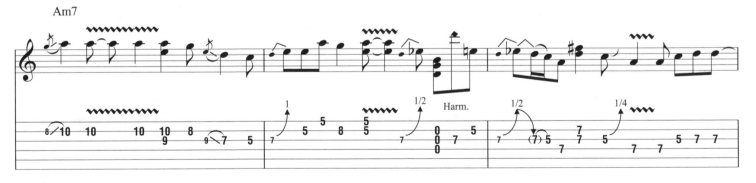

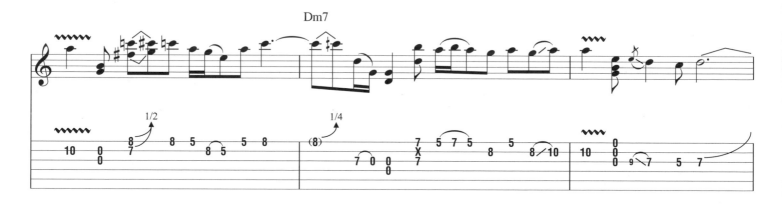

Outro-Guitar Solo

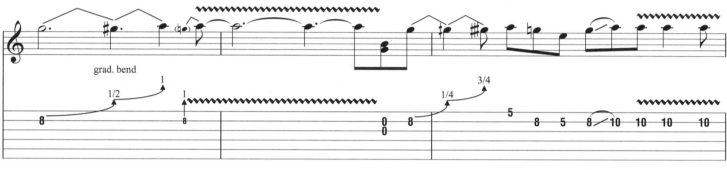

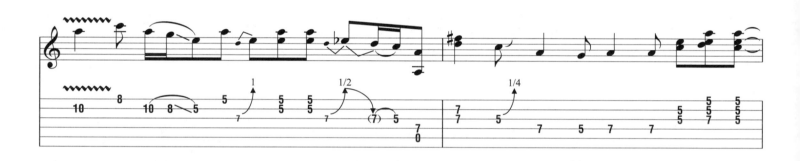

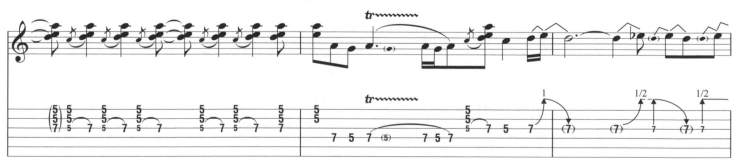

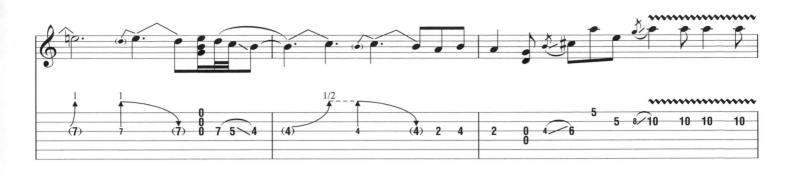

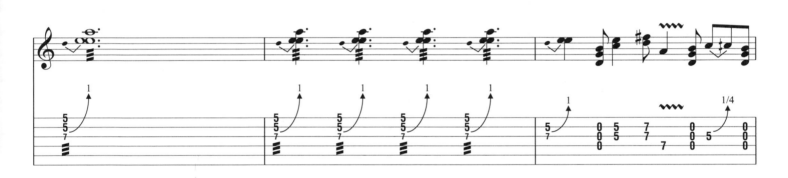

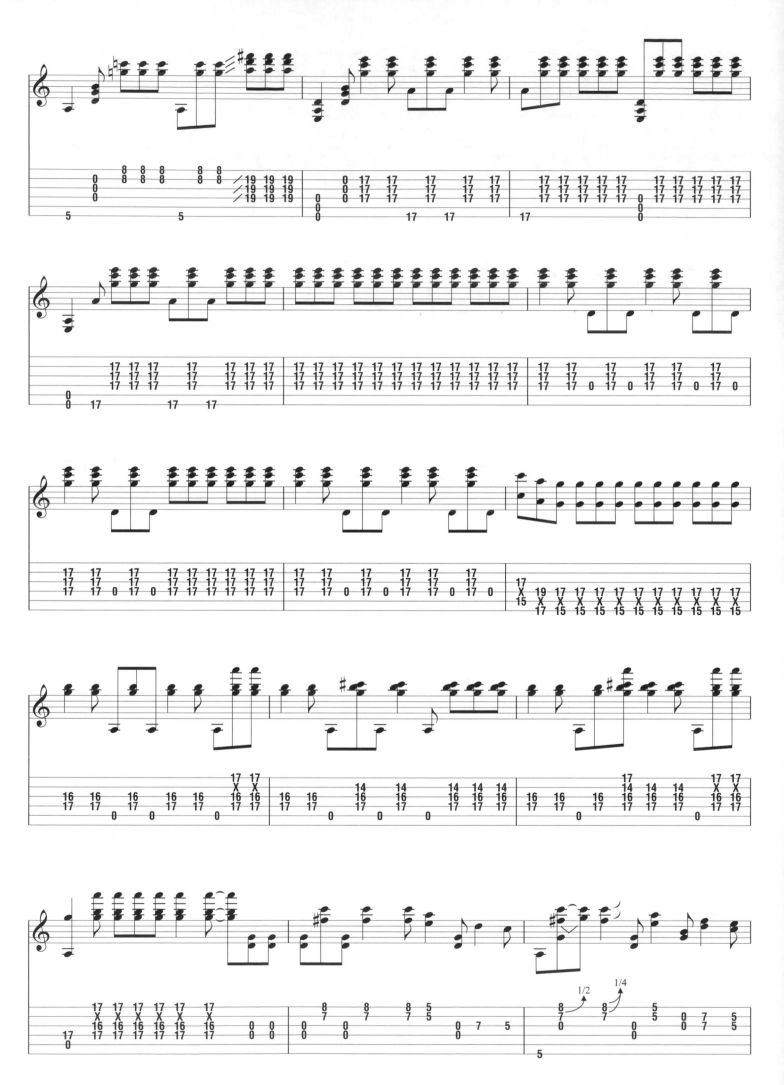

22

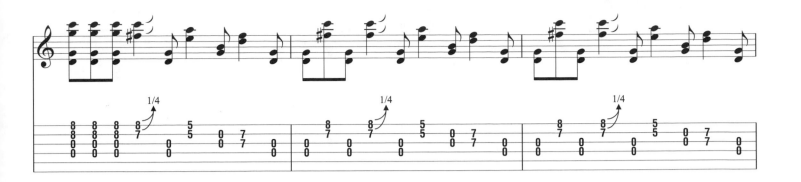

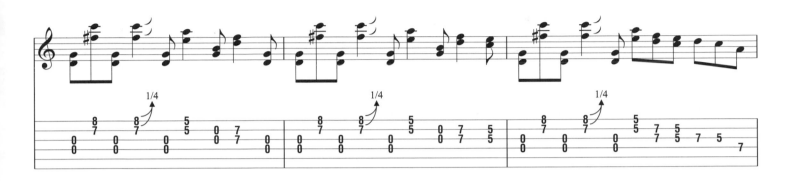

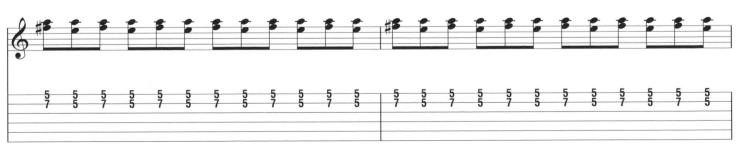

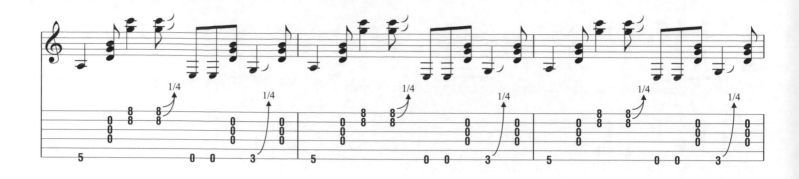

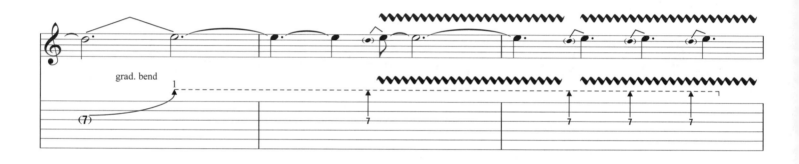

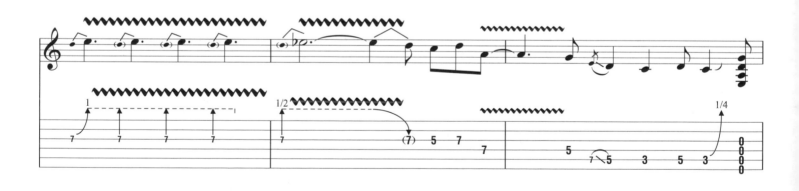

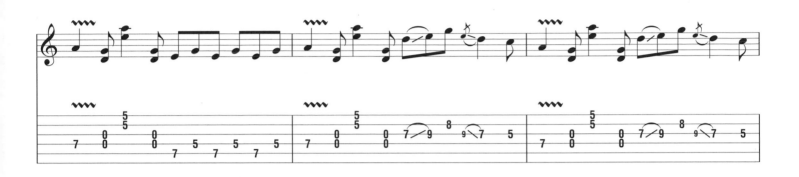

Additional Lyrics

2. Off in the distance, callin' my name,
   I took me a ride on a slow rollin' train.
   It still runs.
   It seems the good die young.
   Playin' on that sad guitar,
   Born with a broken heart.
   Burnin' like a shooting star,
   Born with my broken heart.

3. Seems it was over before it begun.
   Killed by a bullet from a six-string gun.
   Bang a drum.
   Oh, why do the good die young? Yeah.
   Ridin' in a long black car,
   Born with a broken heart.
   Playin' on that sad guitar,
   Born with a broken heart.
   Burnin' like a shootin' star,
   Born with a broken heart.
   Yeah!

Déjà Voodoo

Words and Music by Kenny Wayne Shepherd, Mark Selby and Tia Sillers

Tune down 1/2 step:
(low to high) E♭-A♭-D♭-G♭-B♭-E♭

Intro
Moderately ♩ = 101

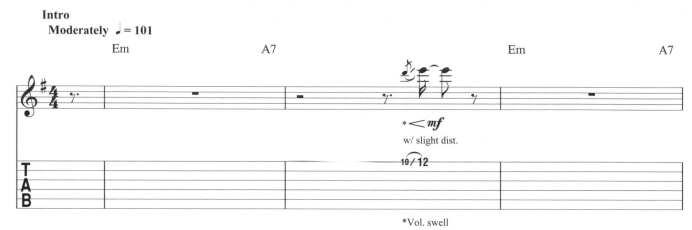

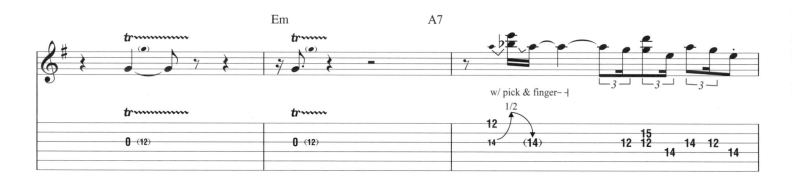

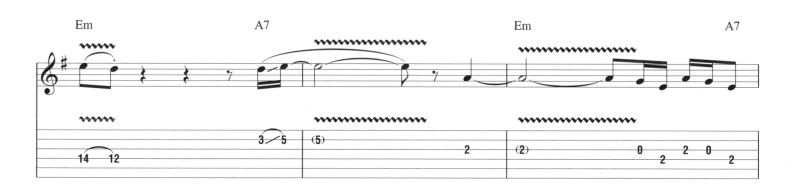

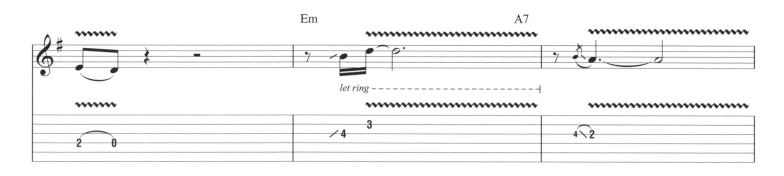

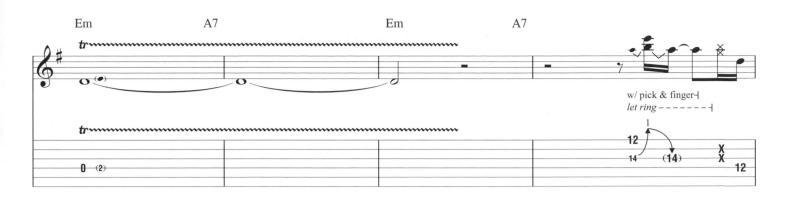

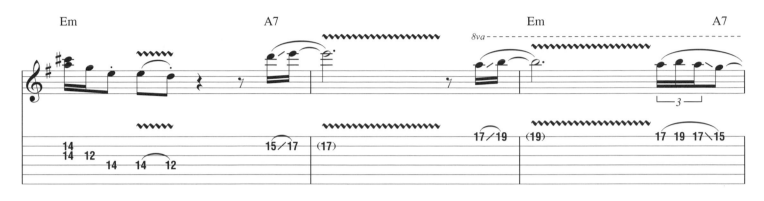

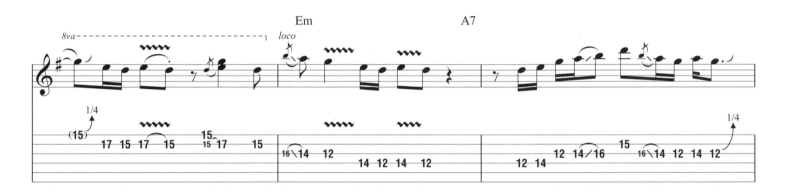

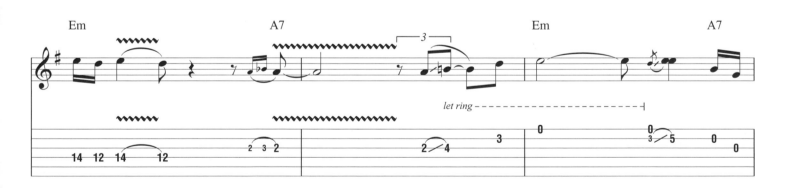

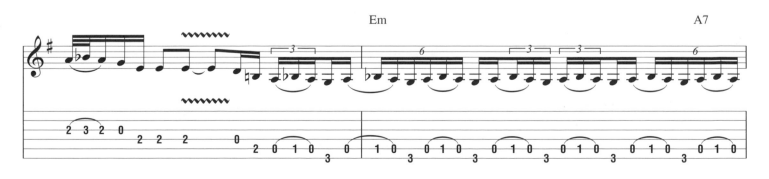

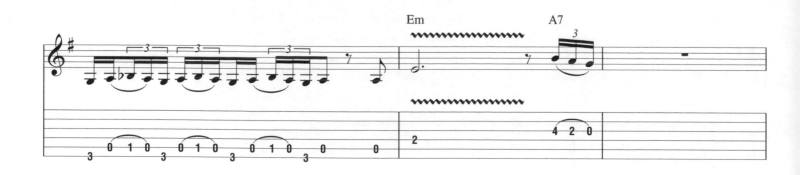

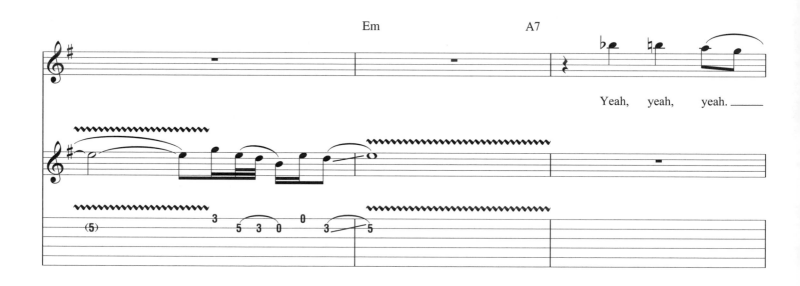

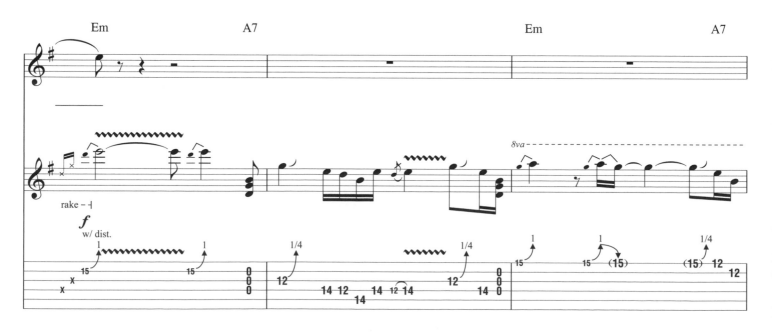

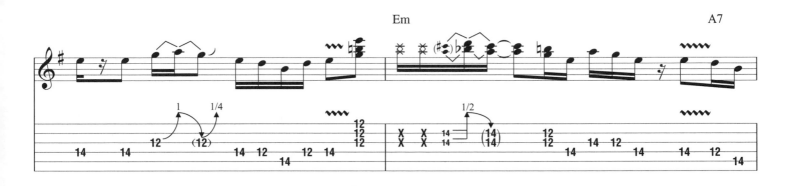

𝄋 Verse

1. Need-les in my heart,

spell on my mind.

2., 3. See additional lyrics

Your pow-er-ful po-tion

Coda 1

Interlude

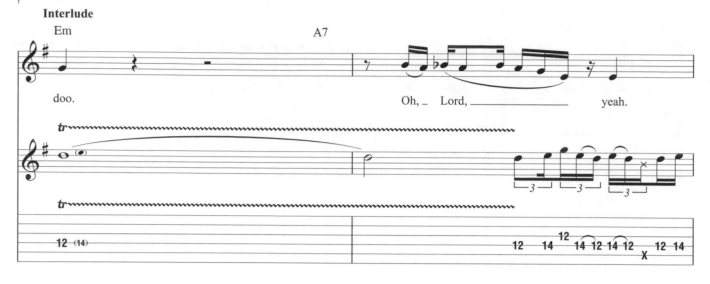

doo.

Oh, _ Lord, _____ yeah.

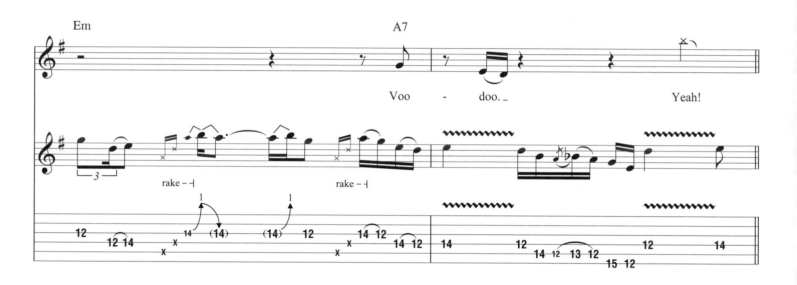

Voo - doo. _   Yeah!

Guitar Solo

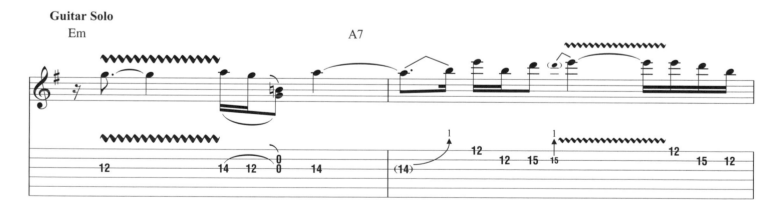

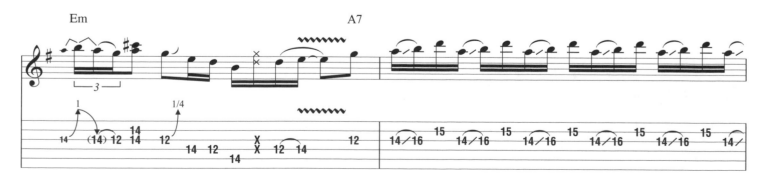

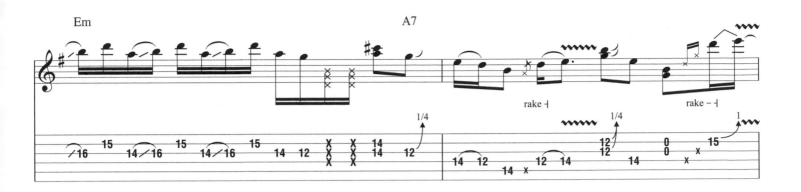

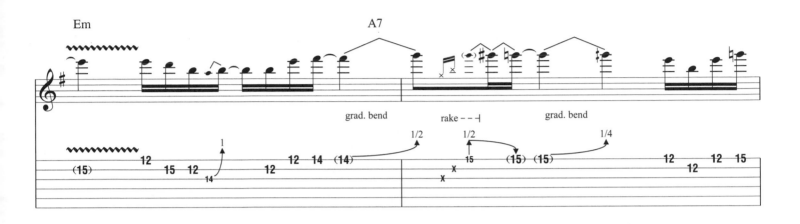

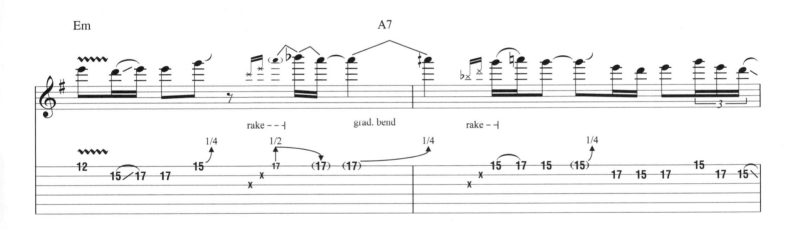

D.S. al Coda 2

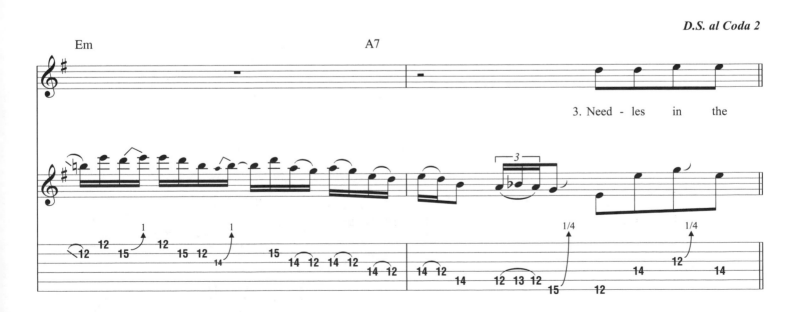

3. Need - les   in   the

Coda 2

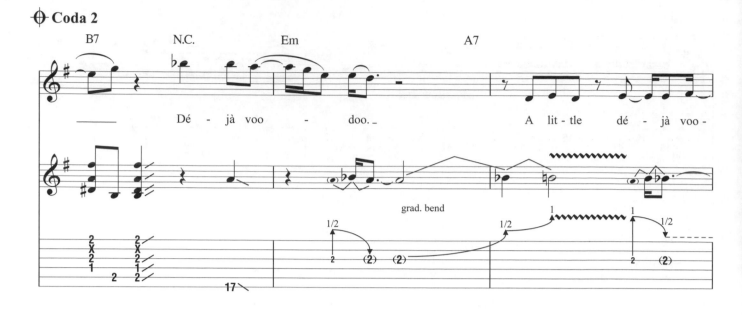

Dé - jà voo - doo._ A lit - tle dé - jà voo-

- doo. 'Jà voo.

Guitar Solo

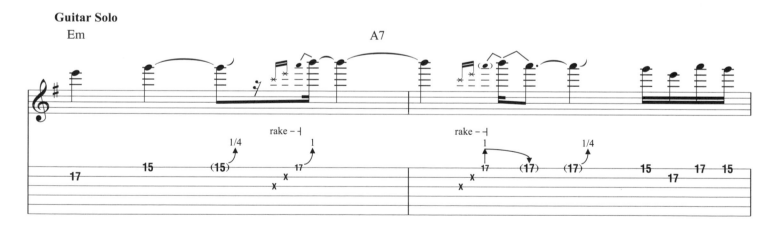

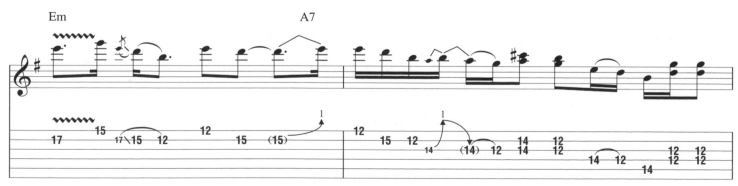

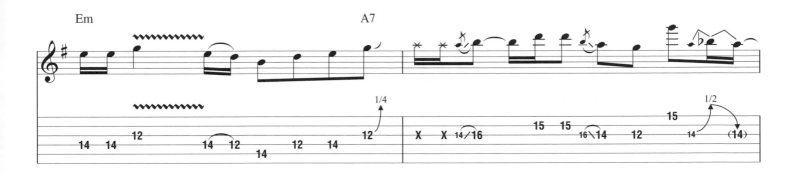

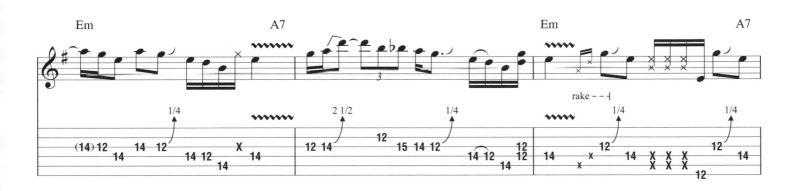

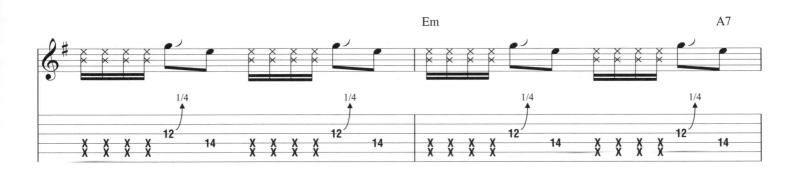

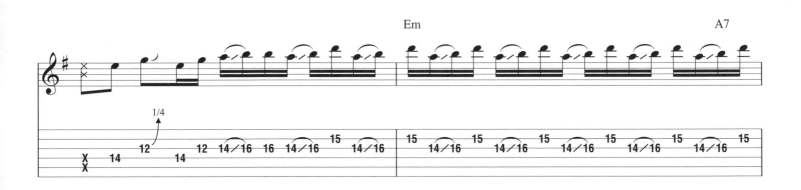

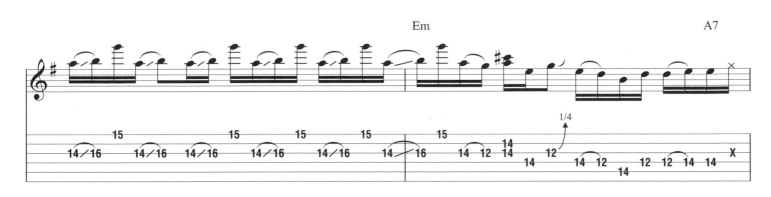

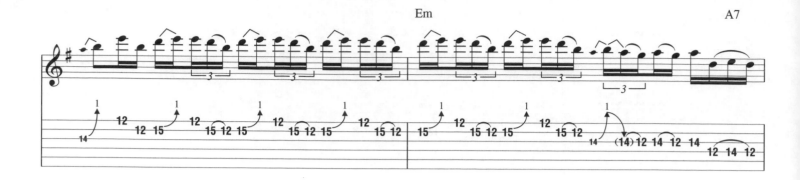

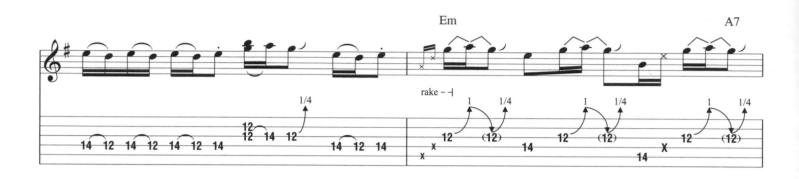

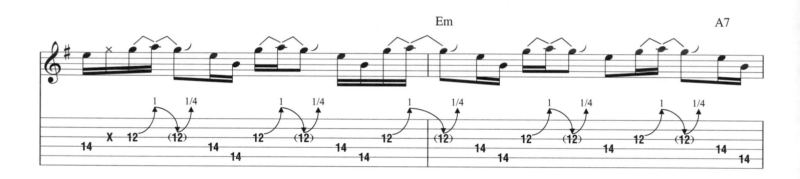

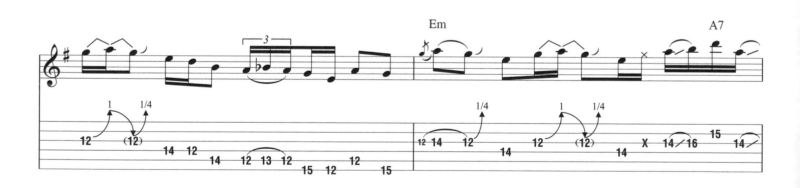

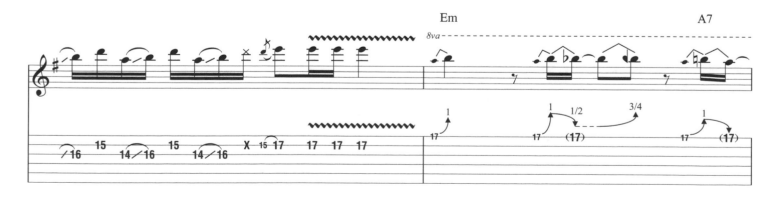

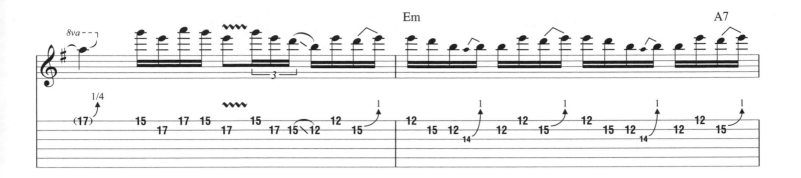

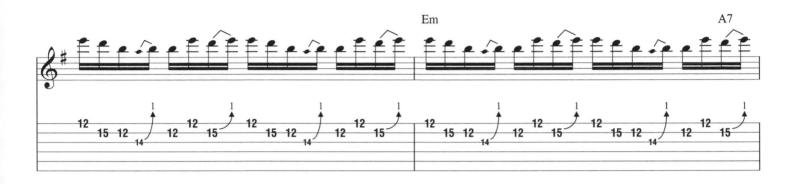

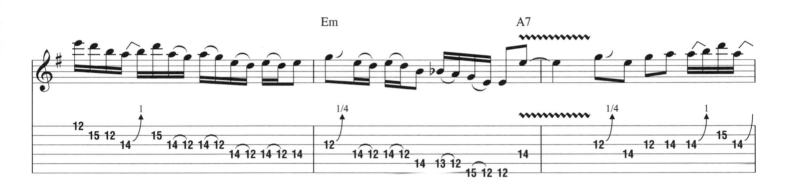

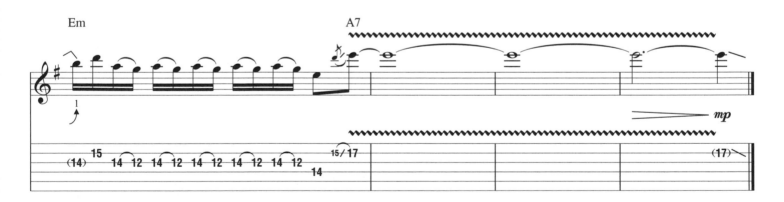

Additional Lyrics

2. Fire in the dark, mm, pounding on my brain, mm.
   Driven by the chant, oo, calling out my name, yeah.
   I toss and turn; I can't sleep.
   Your kiss burns through my dreams.

3. Needles in the dark and swell on my mind.
   Your powerful potion gets me ev'ry time.
   I toss and turn; I can't sleep.
   Your kiss burns through my dreams.

Everything Is Broken

Words and Music by Bob Dylan

Intro
Moderately ♩ = 133

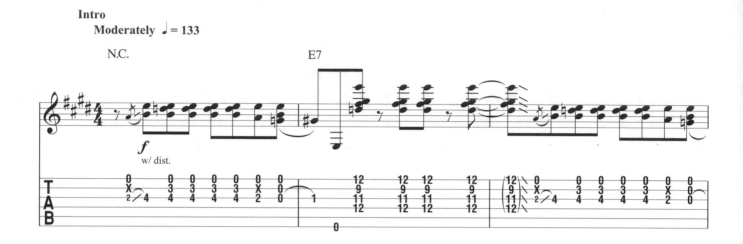

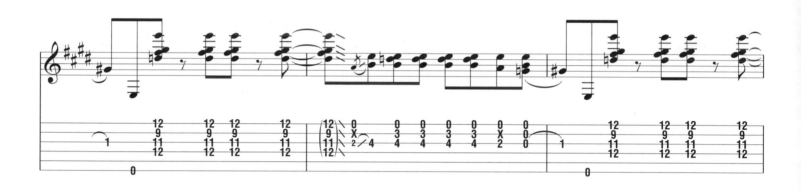

Yeah!

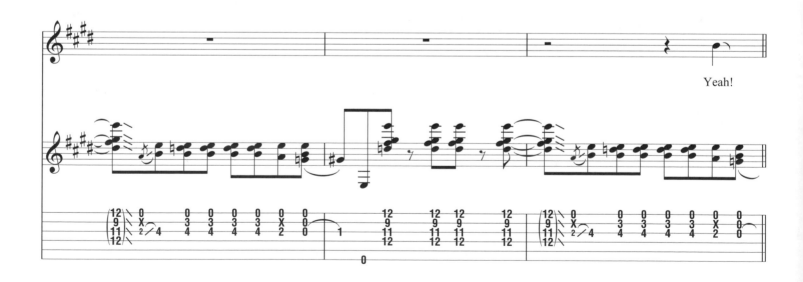

Interlude

D.S. al Coda

$\oplus$ **Coda**

Interlude

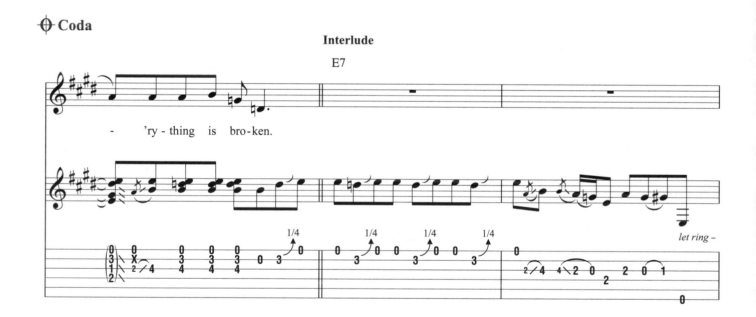

- 'ry - thing   is   bro - ken.

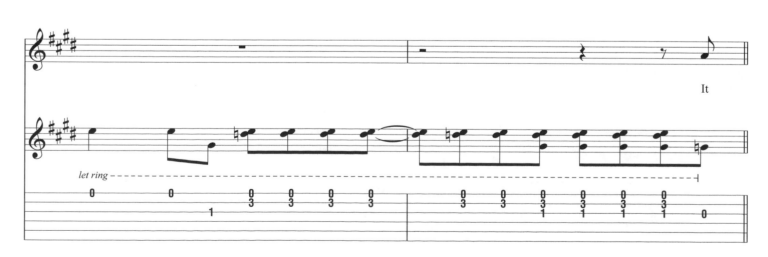

It

bro-ken voic-es ___ on bro-ken phones. ___ Take a deep breath, _

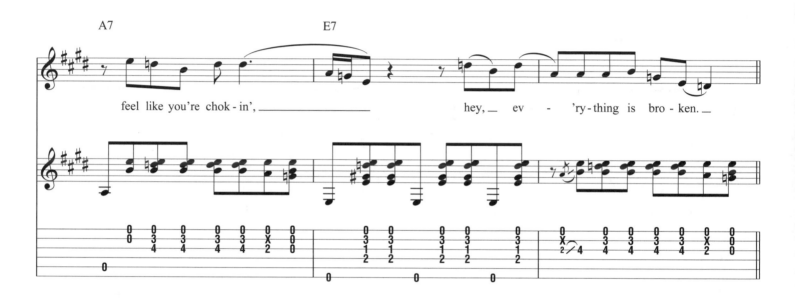

feel like you're chok-in', ___ hey, ___ ev - 'ry-thing is bro-ken. _

Guitar Solo

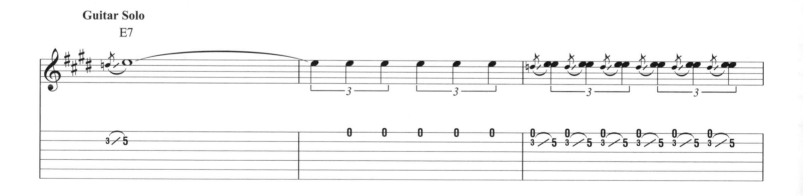

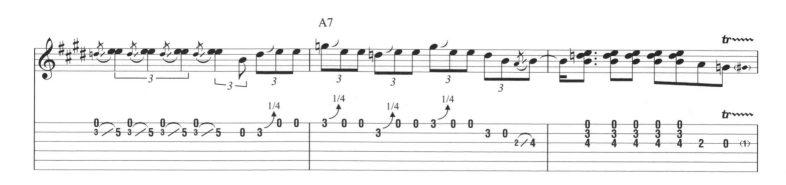

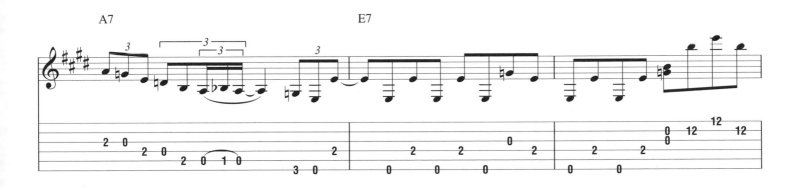

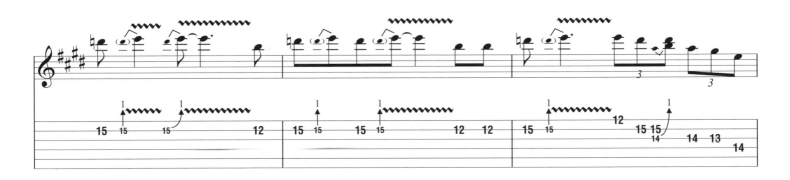

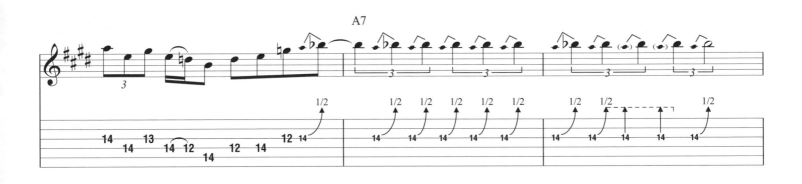

Chorus

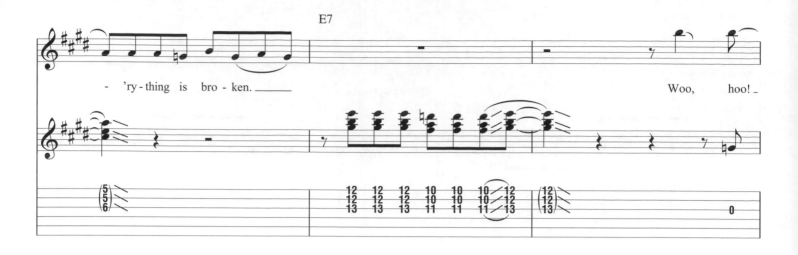

'ry-thing is bro-ken. _____ Woo, hoo! _

Oh, yeah! _____ Oh!

Yeah, ___ ev - 'ry - thing is _____ bro - ken.

Outro-Guitar Solo

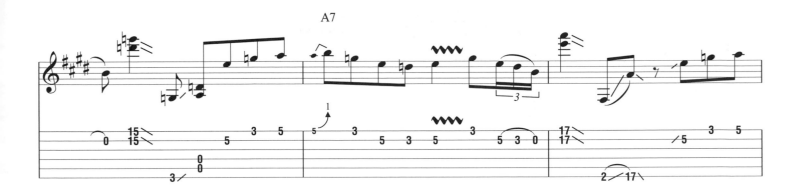

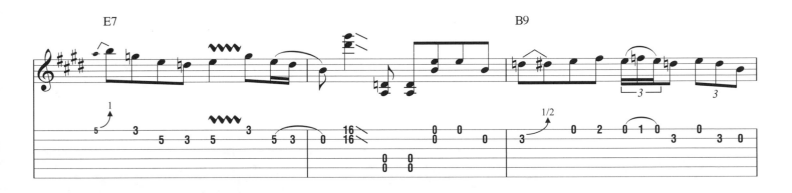

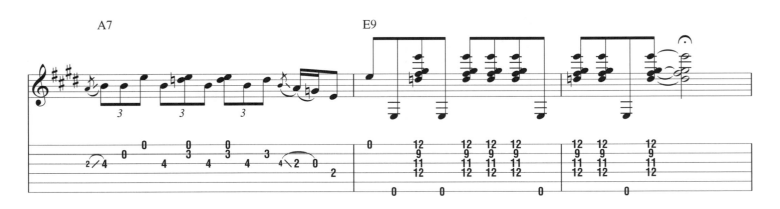

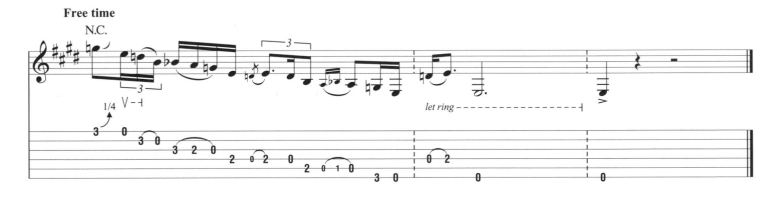

Additional Lyrics

2. Broken bottles, broken legs,
Broken switches, broken gates.
Broken dishes, broken parts.
Yeah, streets are filled with broken hearts.
Broken words, never meant to be spoken.
Oh, ev'rything is broken.

Last Goodbye

Words and Music by Tia Sillers, Mark Selby and Kenny Wayne Shepherd

Capo III

Intro
Slowly ♩ = 75

*Symbols in parentheses represent chord names respective to capoed guitar
and do not reflect actual sounding chords. Capoed fret is "0" in tab.

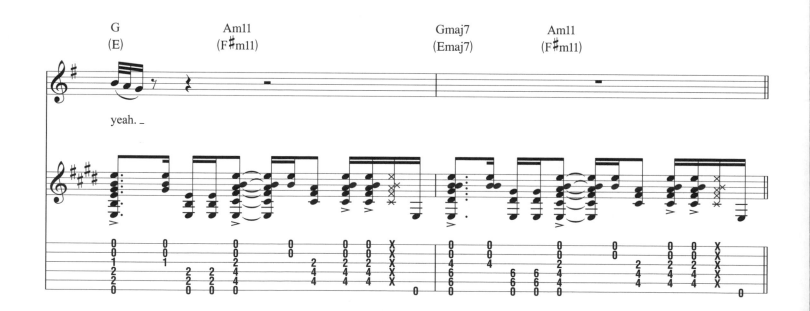

lose ___ my - self,   I could curse   like ___   hell. ___   But I've

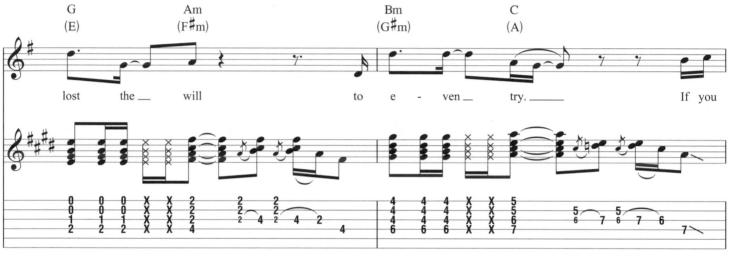

lost   the ___ will   to   e - ven ___   try. _____   If   you

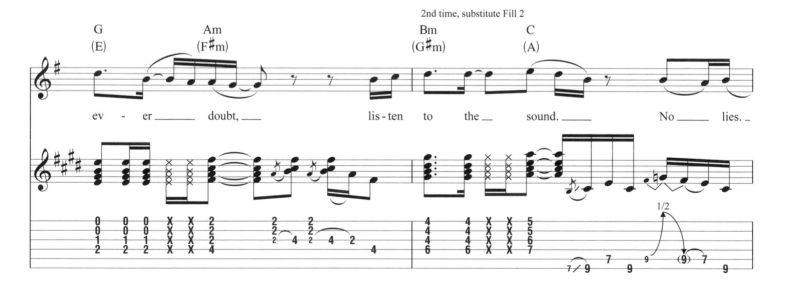

ev - er _____ doubt, ___   lis - ten   to the ___   sound. _____   No _____ lies. _

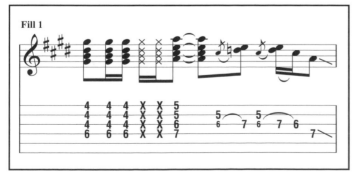

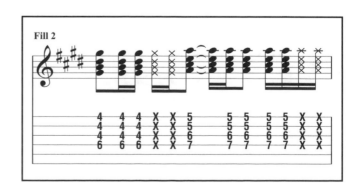

Somehow, Somewhere, Someway

Words and Music by Kenny Wayne Shepherd and Danny Tate

Intro
Moderately ♩ = 112

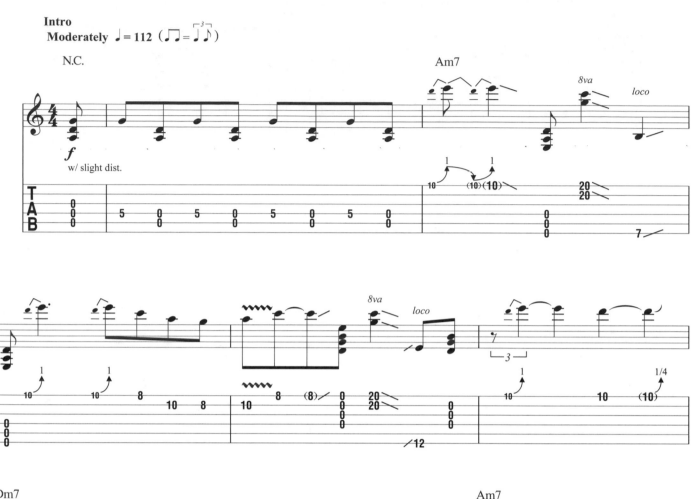

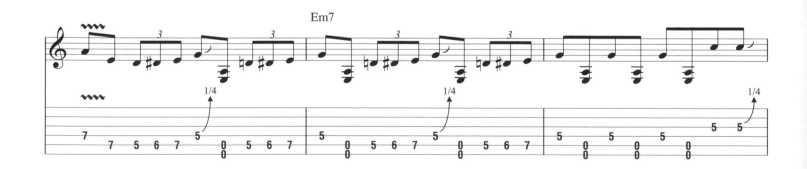

how, some - where, some - way.___ 2. You say I'm real - ly not your

Verse

kind. I know I look ___ a lit - tle rough, ___ now. ___

If I could give you ev - 'ry - thing, ___ girl, ___ would it ev - er be e - nough, ___

___ now? ___ I'll make you mine ___ some - day, ___ some -

Guitar Solo

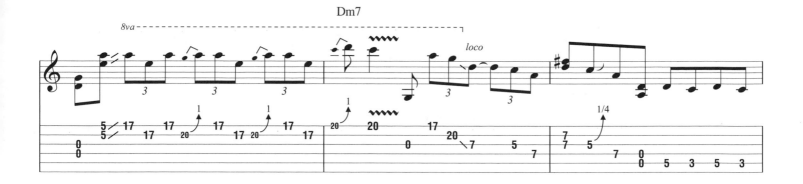

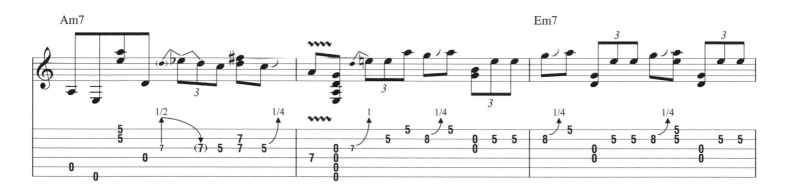

Coda

Verse

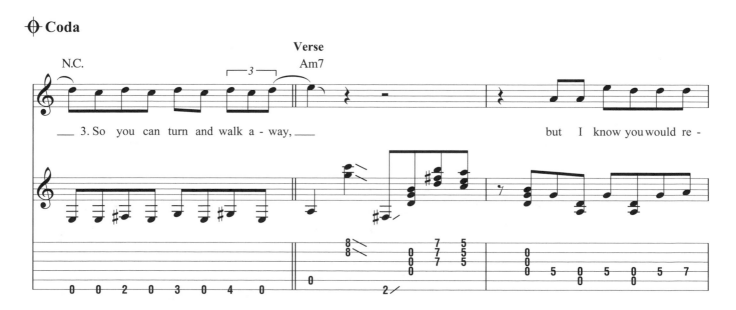

_ 3. So you can turn and walk a - way, _ but I know you would re -

way. _ I'll make _ you mine _ some - day, ___ some -

how, some - where, some - way. _ Oo, yeah. _____

Outro-Guitar Solo

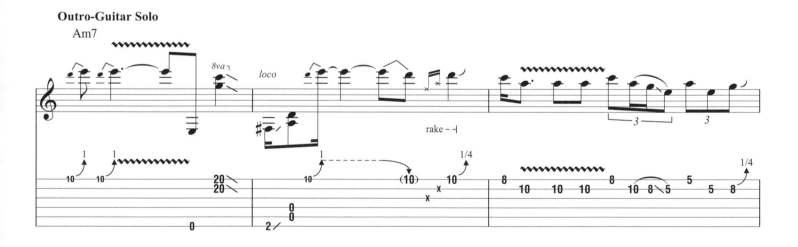

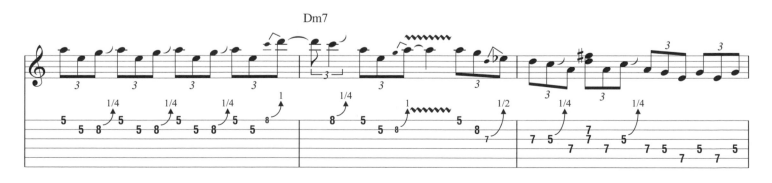

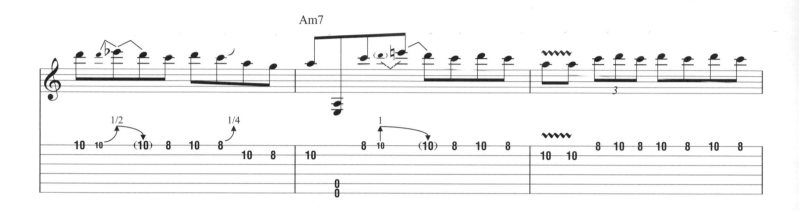

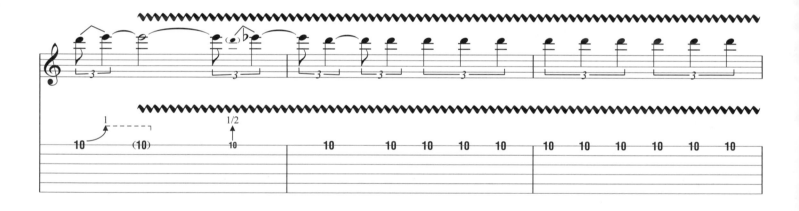

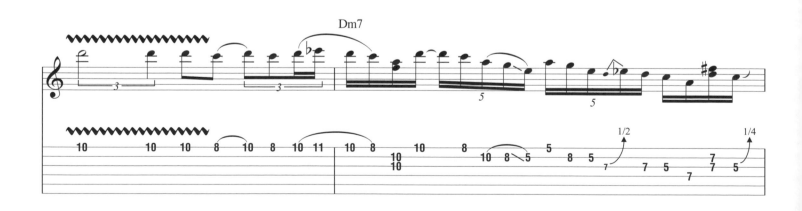

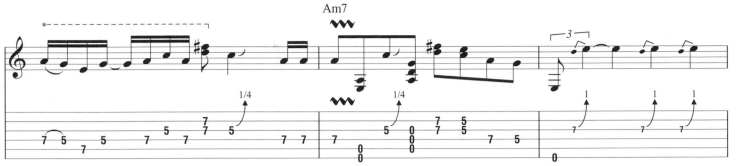

*Played behind the beat.

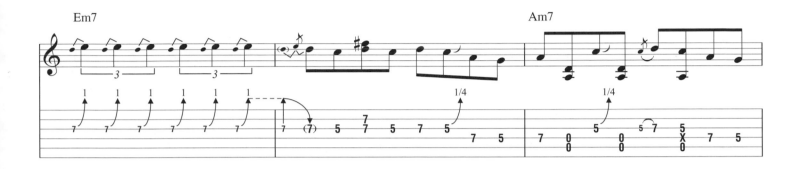

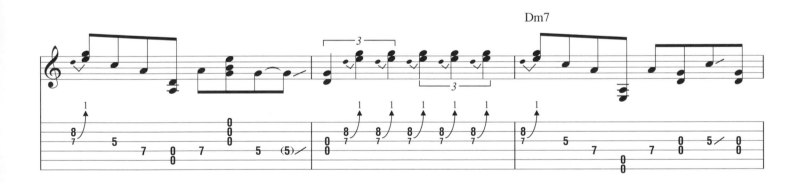

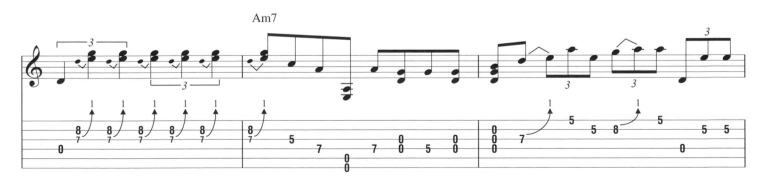

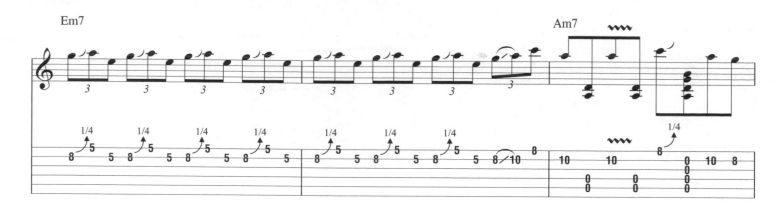

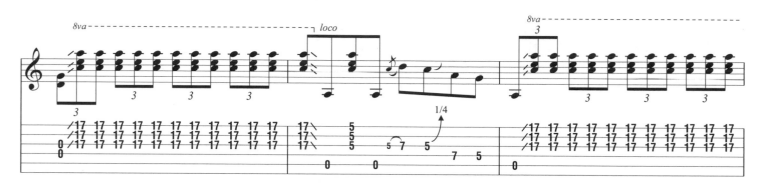

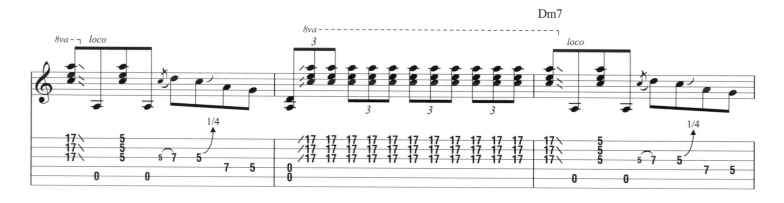

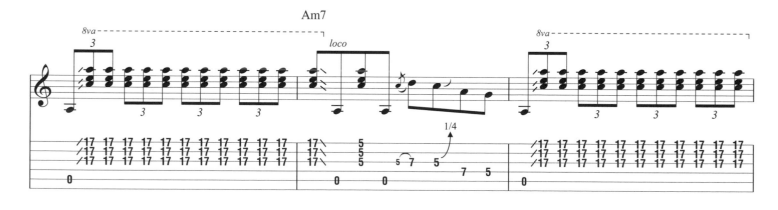

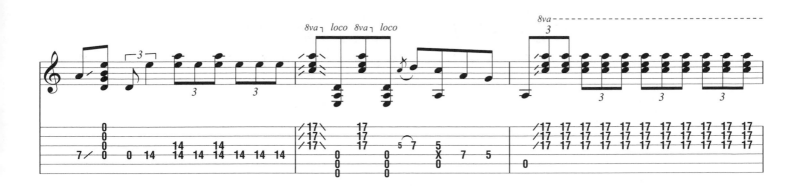

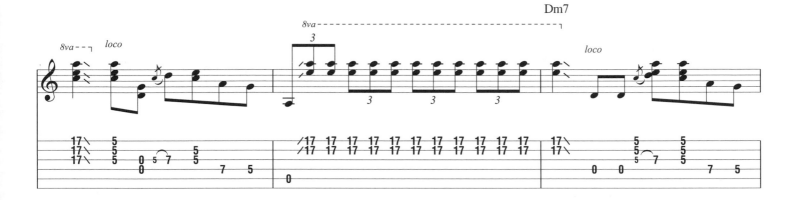

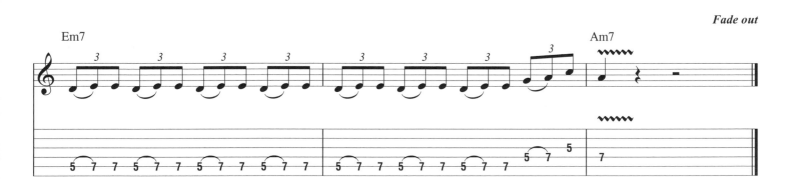

Additional Lyrics

Bridge Oh, don't you wonder what's goin' on, baby,
When the night rolls in?
And somethin' happens that feels so strong and,
And it will happen again.

Never Lookin' Back

Words and Music by Kenny Wayne Shepherd, Tia Sillers and Mark Selby

E5/B   B5   B

And I'm nev - er look - in' back.

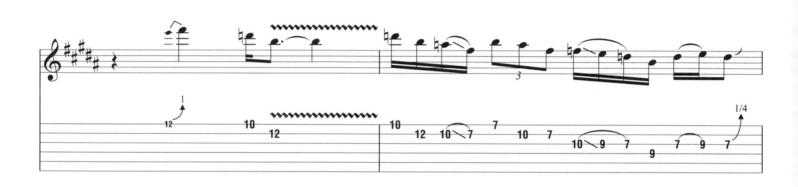

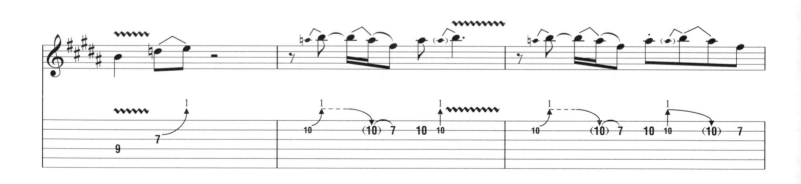

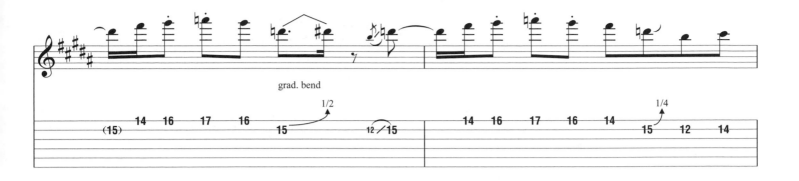

grad. bend

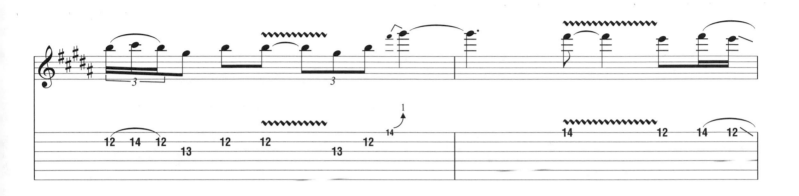

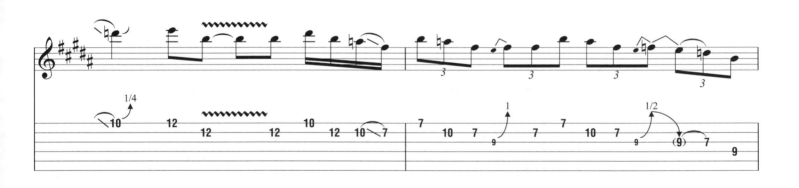

D5

Watch out.

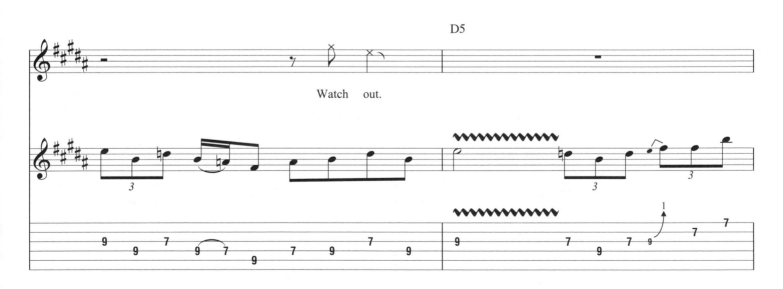

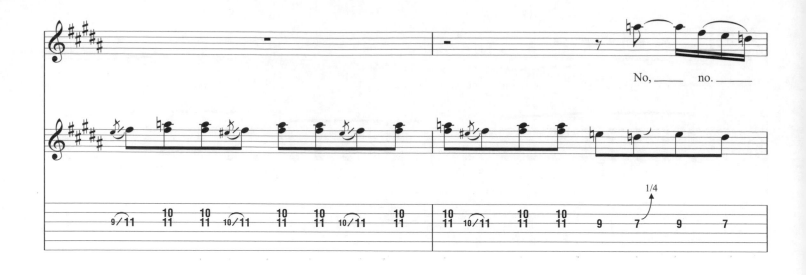

No, _____ no. _____

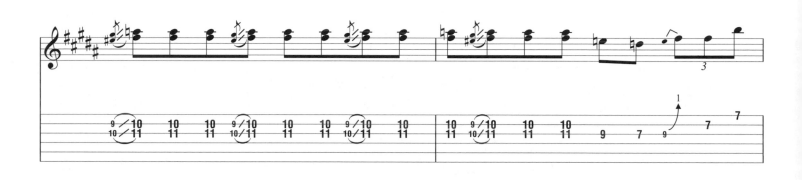

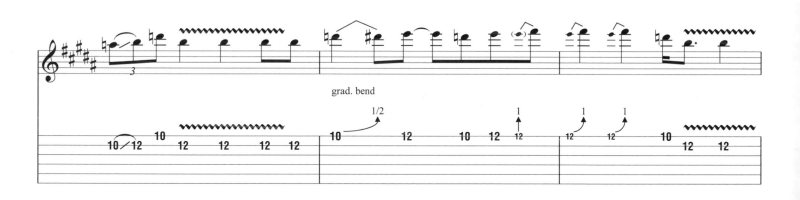

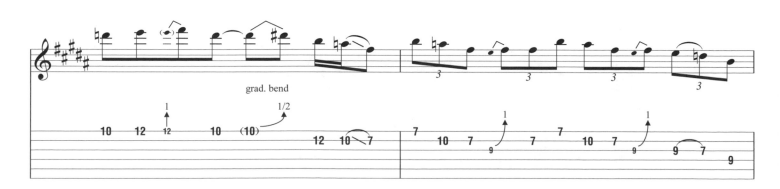

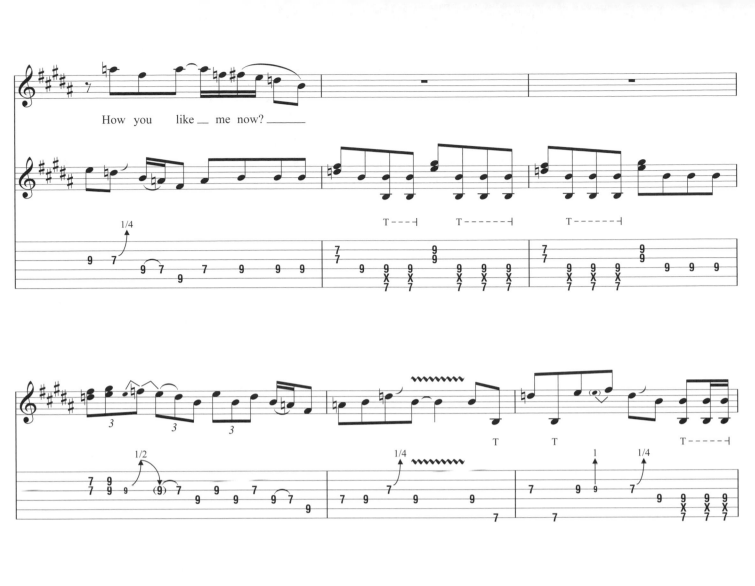

How you   like __ me now? _____

Yeah. _____   Woo!

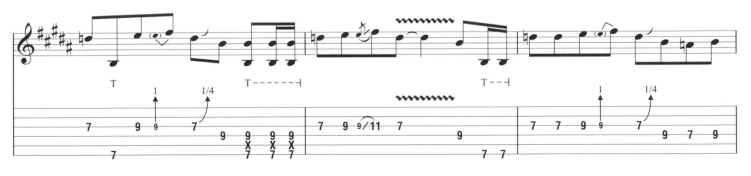

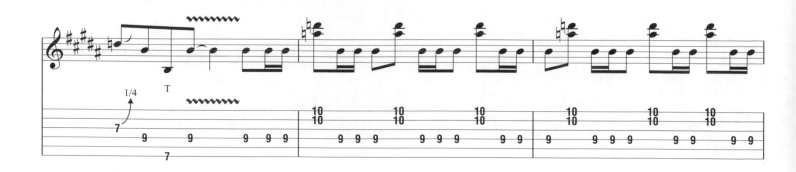

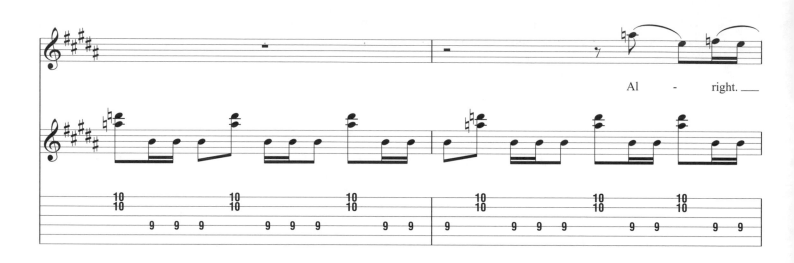

Al - right. __

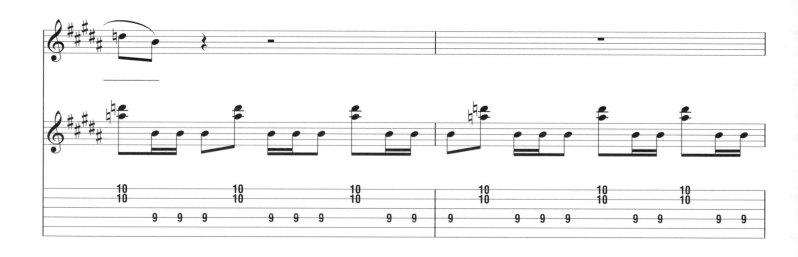

Yeah! _____ Woo!

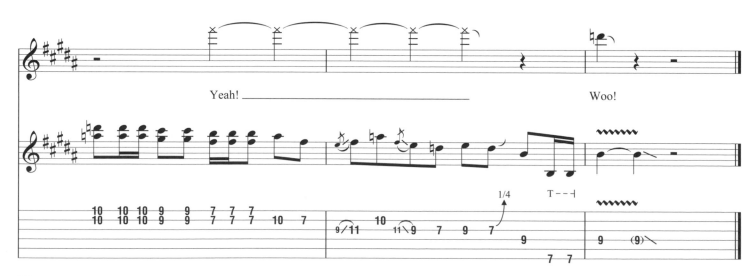

True Lies

Words and Music by Kenny Wayne Shepherd and Danny Tate

1. Now, where do you go af-ter mid — night,

true _____ lies. _____

2. Hey,

Verse

some-one's been sleep-in' in my bed, _

'cause this room don't smell like you and me. _____

Some-one's been sneak-in' out the win-dow.

Do you think I'm too blind to see ____ when you

look me in the eye ____ and make it sound so ver-y nice ____ with your

true _____ lies. ____ It was a

clev - er dis - guise ____ but, girl, _ I'm get - tin' wise ____ to your

word gets in the wind,___ then it's bound__ to blow back a - round._____

Guitar Solo

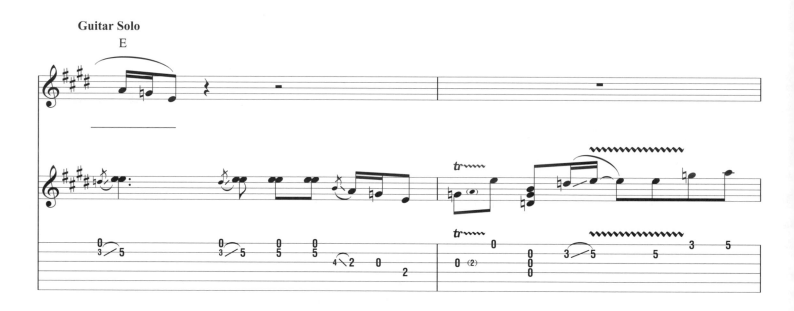

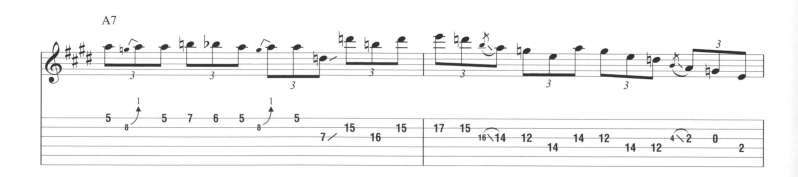

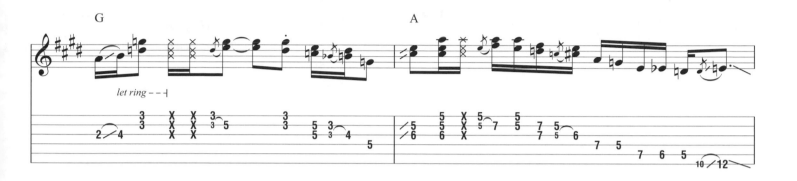

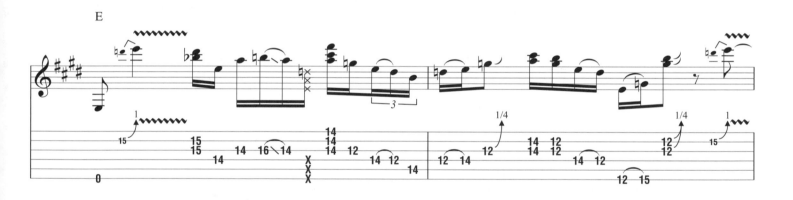

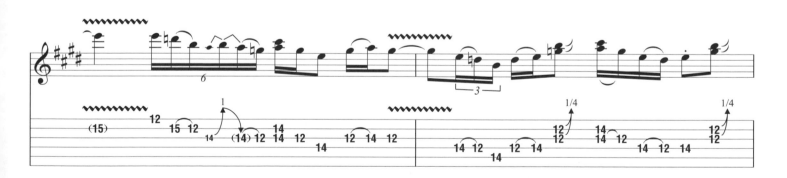

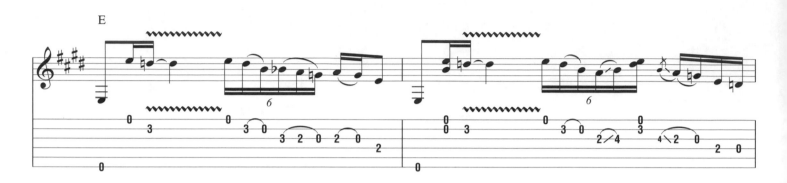

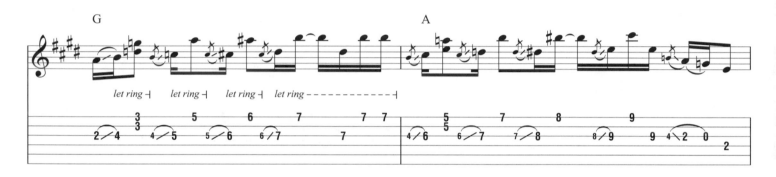

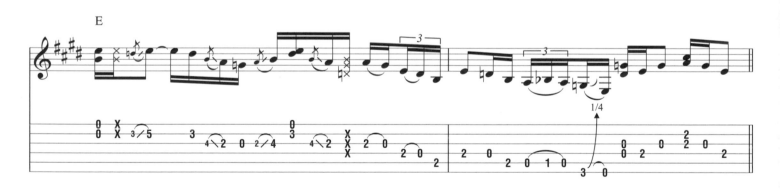

Verse

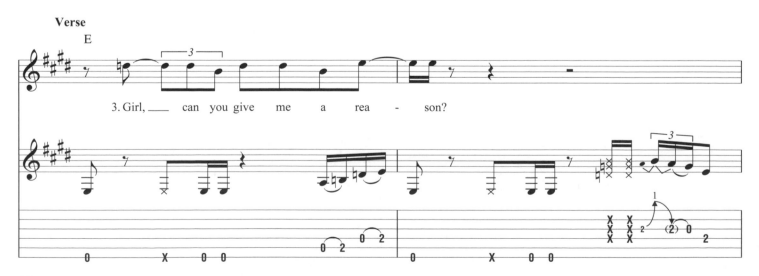

3. Girl, ___ can you give me a rea - son?

I bet __ you don't e - ven know why. ___

'Cause I can't fig - ure out what __ you're think - in' or

what it is __ you try - in' to jus - ti - fy. ___ Hey, when you

look me in the eye __ and make it sound so ver - y nice __ with your

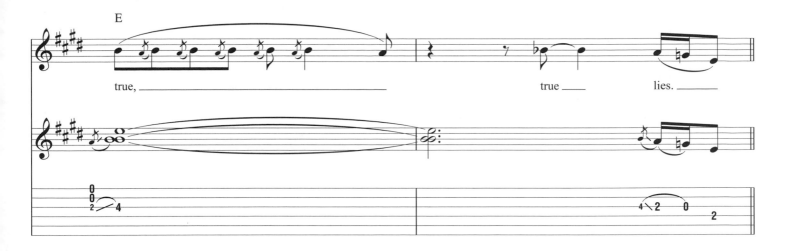

true,_____ true___ lies.____

Interlude

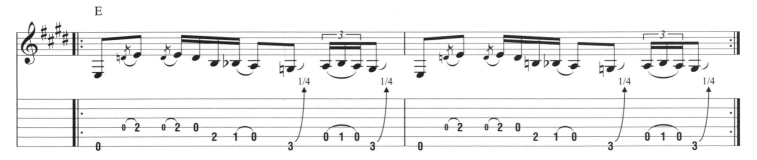

Guitar Solo

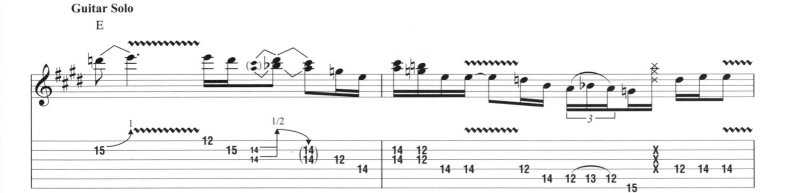

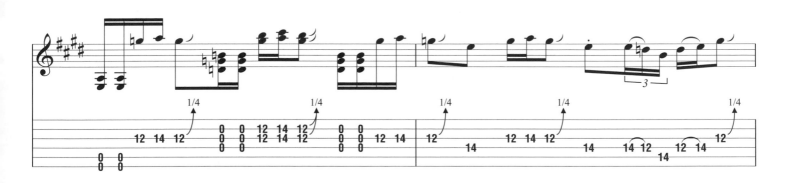

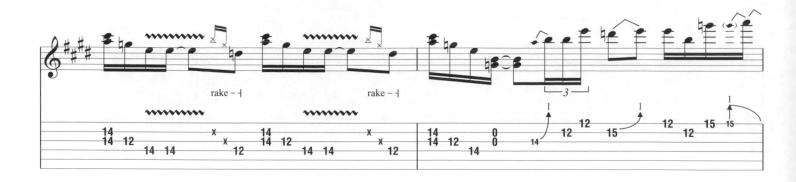

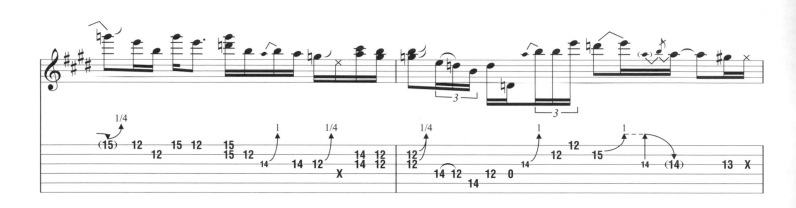

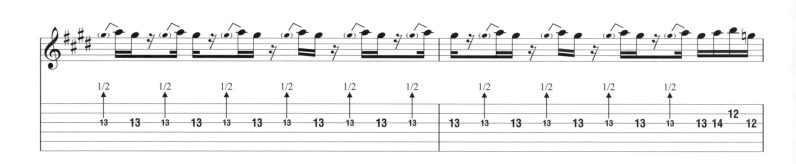

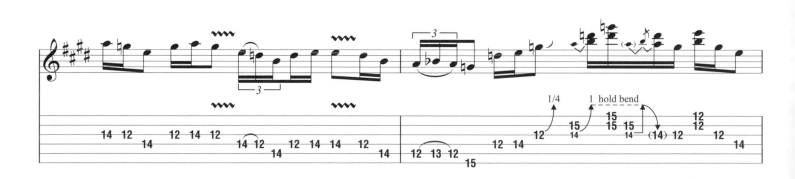

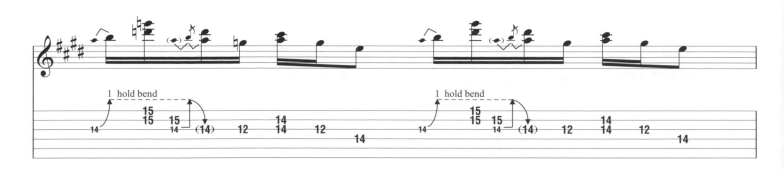

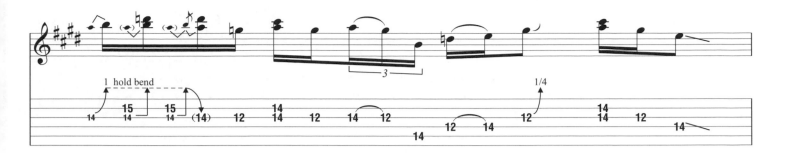

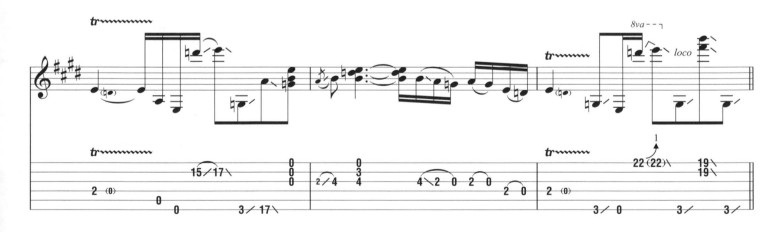

Outro

E

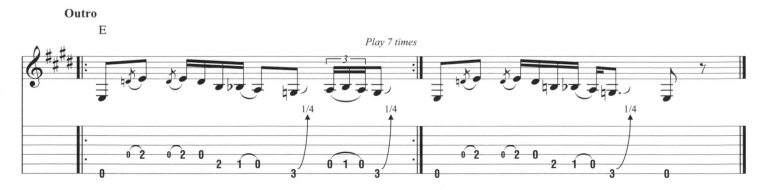

HAL•LEONARD GUITAR PLAY-ALONG

This series will help you play your favorite songs quickly and easily. Just follow the tab and listen to the CD to the hear how the guitar should sound, and then play along using the separate backing tracks. Mac or PC users can also slow down the tempo without changing pitch by using the CD in their computer. The melody and lyrics are included in the book so that you can sing or simply follow along.

INCLUDES TAB

VOL. 1 – ROCK	00699570 / $16.99	
VOL. 2 – ACOUSTIC	00699569 / $16.95	
VOL. 3 – HARD ROCK	00699573 / $16.95	
VOL. 4 – POP/ROCK	00699571 / $16.99	
VOL. 5 – MODERN ROCK	00699574 / $16.99	
VOL. 6 – '90S ROCK	00699572 / $16.99	
VOL. 7 – BLUES	00699575 / $16.95	
VOL. 8 – ROCK	00699585 / $14.99	
VOL. 9 – PUNK ROCK	00699576 / $14.95	
VOL. 10 – ACOUSTIC	00699586 / $16.95	
VOL. 11 – EARLY ROCK	00699579 / $14.95	
VOL. 12 – POP/ROCK	00699587 / $14.95	
VOL. 13 – FOLK ROCK	00699581 / $15.99	
VOL. 14 – BLUES ROCK	00699582 / $16.95	
VOL. 15 – R&B	00699583 / $14.95	
VOL. 16 – JAZZ	00699584 / $15.95	
VOL. 17 – COUNTRY	00699588 / $15.95	
VOL. 18 – ACOUSTIC ROCK	00699577 / $15.95	
VOL. 19 – SOUL	00699578 / $14.99	
VOL. 20 – ROCKABILLY	00699580 / $14.95	
VOL. 21 – YULETIDE	00699602 / $14.95	
VOL. 22 – CHRISTMAS	00699600 / $15.95	
VOL. 23 – SURF	00699635 / $14.95	
VOL. 24 – ERIC CLAPTON	00699649 / $17.99	
VOL. 25 – LENNON & MCCARTNEY	00699642 / $16.99	
VOL. 26 – ELVIS PRESLEY	00699643 / $14.95	
VOL. 27 – DAVID LEE ROTH	00699645 / $16.95	
VOL. 28 – GREG KOCH	00699646 / $14.95	
VOL. 29 – BOB SEGER	00699647 / $15.99	
VOL. 30 – KISS	00699644 / $16.99	
VOL. 31 – CHRISTMAS HITS	00699652 / $14.95	
VOL. 32 – THE OFFSPRING	00699653 / $14.95	
VOL. 33 – ACOUSTIC CLASSICS	00699656 / $16.95	
VOL. 34 – CLASSIC ROCK	00699658 / $16.95	
VOL. 35 – HAIR METAL	00699660 / $16.95	
VOL. 36 – SOUTHERN ROCK	00699661 / $16.95	
VOL. 37 – ACOUSTIC UNPLUGGED	00699662 / $22.99	
VOL. 38 – BLUES	00699663 / $16.95	
VOL. 39 – '80S METAL	00699664 / $16.99	
VOL. 40 – INCUBUS	00699668 / $17.95	
VOL. 41 – ERIC CLAPTON	00699669 / $16.95	
VOL. 42 – 2000S ROCK	00699670 / $16.99	
VOL. 43 – LYNYRD SKYNYRD	00699681 / $17.95	
VOL. 44 – JAZZ	00699689 / $14.99	
VOL. 45 – TV THEMES	00699718 / $14.95	
VOL. 46 – MAINSTREAM ROCK	00699722 / $16.95	
VOL. 47 – HENDRIX SMASH HITS	00699723 / $19.95	
VOL. 48 – AEROSMITH CLASSICS	00699724 / $17.99	
VOL. 49 – STEVIE RAY VAUGHAN	00699725 / $17.99	
VOL. 51 – ALTERNATIVE '90S	00699727 / $14.99	
VOL. 52 – FUNK	00699728 / $14.95	
VOL. 53 – DISCO	00699729 / $14.99	
VOL. 54 – HEAVY METAL	00699730 / $14.95	
VOL. 55 – POP METAL	00699731 / $14.95	
VOL. 56 – FOO FIGHTERS	00699749 / $15.99	
VOL. 57 – SYSTEM OF A DOWN	00699751 / $14.95	
VOL. 58 – BLINK-182	00699772 / $14.95	
VOL. 59 – CHET ATKINS	00702347 / $16.99	
VOL. 60 – 3 DOORS DOWN	00699774 / $14.95	
VOL. 61 – SLIPKNOT	00699775 / $16.99	
VOL. 62 – CHRISTMAS CAROLS	00699798 / $12.95	
VOL. 63 – CREEDENCE CLEARWATER REVIVAL	00699802 / $16.99	
VOL. 64 – THE ULTIMATE OZZY OSBOURNE	00699803 / $16.99	
VOL. 66 – THE ROLLING STONES	00699807 / $16.95	
VOL. 67 – BLACK SABBATH	00699808 / $16.99	
VOL. 68 – PINK FLOYD – DARK SIDE OF THE MOON	00699809 / $16.99	
VOL. 69 – ACOUSTIC FAVORITES	00699810 / $14.95	
VOL. 70 – OZZY OSBOURNE	00699805 / $16.99	
VOL. 71 – CHRISTIAN ROCK	00699824 / $14.95	
VOL. 73 – BLUESY ROCK	00699829 / $16.99	
VOL. 75 – TOM PETTY	00699882 / $16.99	
VOL. 76 – COUNTRY HITS	00699884 / $14.95	
VOL. 77 – BLUEGRASS	00699910 / $14.99	
VOL. 78 – NIRVANA	00700132 / $16.99	
VOL. 79 – NEIL YOUNG	00700133 / $24.99	
VOL. 80 – ACOUSTIC ANTHOLOGY	00700175 / $19.95	
VOL. 81 – ROCK ANTHOLOGY	00700176 / $22.99	
VOL. 82 – EASY SONGS	00700177 / $12.99	
VOL. 83 – THREE CHORD SONGS	00700178 / $16.99	
VOL. 84 – STEELY DAN	00700200 / $16.99	
VOL. 85 – THE POLICE	00700269 / $16.99	
VOL. 86 – BOSTON	00700465 / $16.99	
VOL. 87 – ACOUSTIC WOMEN	00700763 / $14.99	
VOL. 88 – GRUNGE	00700467 / $16.99	
VOL. 89 – REGGAE	00700468 / $15.99	
VOL. 90 – CLASSICAL POP	00700469 / $14.99	
VOL. 91 – BLUES INSTRUMENTALS	00700505 / $14.99	
VOL. 92 – EARLY ROCK INSTRUMENTALS	00700506 / $14.99	
VOL. 93 – ROCK INSTRUMENTALS	00700507 / $16.99	
VOL. 95 – BLUES CLASSICS	00700509 / $14.99	
VOL. 96 – THIRD DAY	00700560 / $14.95	
VOL. 97 – ROCK BAND	00700703 / $14.99	
VOL. 99 – ZZ TOP	00700762 / $16.99	
VOL. 100 – B.B. KING	00700466 / $16.99	
VOL. 101 – SONGS FOR BEGINNERS	00701917 / $14.99	
VOL. 102 – CLASSIC PUNK	00700769 / $14.99	
VOL. 103 – SWITCHFOOT	00700773 / $16.99	
VOL. 104 – DUANE ALLMAN	00700846 / $16.99	
VOL. 106 – WEEZER	00700958 / $14.99	
VOL. 107 – CREAM	00701069 / $16.99	
VOL. 108 – THE WHO	00701053 / $16.99	
VOL. 109 – STEVE MILLER	00701054 / $14.99	
VOL. 111 – JOHN MELLENCAMP	00701056 / $14.99	
VOL. 112 – QUEEN	00701052 / $16.99	
VOL. 113 – JIM CROCE	00701058 / $15.99	
VOL. 114 – BON JOVI	00701060 / $14.99	
VOL. 115 – JOHNNY CASH	00701070 / $16.99	
VOL. 116 – THE VENTURES	00701124 / $14.99	
VOL. 117 – BRAD PAISLEY	00701224/ $16.99	
VOL. 118 – ERIC JOHNSON	00701353 / $16.99	
VOL. 119 – AC/DC CLASSICS	00701356 / $17.99	
VOL. 120 – PROGRESSIVE ROCK	00701457 / $14.99	
VOL. 121 – U2	00701508 / $16.99	
VOL. 123 – LENNON & MCCARTNEY ACOUSTIC	00701614 / $16.99	
VOL. 124 – MODERN WORSHIP	00701629 / $14.99	
VOL. 125 – JEFF BECK	00701687 / $16.99	
VOL. 126 – BOB MARLEY	00701701 / $16.99	
VOL. 127 – 1970S ROCK	00701739 / $14.99	
VOL. 128 – 1960S ROCK	00701740 / $14.99	
VOL. 129 – MEGADETH	00701741 / $16.99	
VOL. 131 – 1990S ROCK	00701743 / $14.99	
VOL. 132 – COUNTRY ROCK	00701757 / $15.99	
VOL. 133 – TAYLOR SWIFT	00701894 / $16.99	
VOL. 134 – AVENGED SEVENFOLD	00701906 / $16.99	
VOL. 136 – GUITAR THEMES	00701922 / $14.99	
VOL. 137 – IRISH TUNES	00701966 / $15.99	
VOL. 138 – BLUEGRASS CLASSICS	00701967 / $14.99	
VOL. 139 – GARY MOORE	00702370 / $16.99	
VOL. 140 – MORE STEVIE RAY VAUGHAN	00702396 / $17.99	
VOL. 141 – ACOUSTIC HITS	00702401 / $16.99	
VOL. 142 – KINGS OF LEON	00702418 / $16.99	
VOL. 144 – DJANGO REINHARDT	00702531 / $16.99	
VOL. 145 – DEF LEPPARD	00702532 / $16.99	
VOL. 147 – SIMON & GARFUNKEL	14041591 / $16.99	
VOL. 148 – BOB DYLAN	14041592 / $16.99	
VOL. 149 – AC/DC HITS	14041593 / $17.99	
VOL. 150 – ZAKK WYLDE	02501717 / $16.99	
VOL. 153 – RED HOT CHILI PEPPERS	00702990 / $19.99	
VOL. 156 – SLAYER	00703770 / $17.99	
VOL. 157 – FLEETWOOD MAC	00101382 / $16.99	
VOL. 158 – ULTIMATE CHRISTMAS	00101889 / $14.99	
VOL. 160 – T-BONE WALKER	00102641 / $16.99	
VOL. 161 – THE EAGLES – ACOUSTIC	00102659 / $17.99	
VOL. 162 – THE EAGLES HITS	00102667 / $17.99	
VOL. 163 – PANTERA	00103036 / $17.99	
VOL. 166 – MODERN BLUES	00700764 / $16.99	
VOL. 168 – KISS	00113421 / $16.99	
VOL. 169 – TAYLOR SWIFT	00115982 / $16.99	
VOL. 170 – THREE DAYS GRACE	00117337 / $16.99	
VOL. 172 – THE DOOBIE BROTHERS	00119670 / $16.99	
VOL. 174 – SCORPIONS	00122119 / $16.99	
VOL. 176 – BLUES BREAKERS WITH JOHN MAYALL & ERIC CLAPTON	00122132 / $19.99	
VOL. 177 – ALBERT KING	00123271 / $16.99	
VOL. 178 – JASON MRAZ	00124165 / $17.99	

Complete song lists available online.

Prices, contents, and availability subject to change without notice.

HAL•LEONARD® CORPORATION

7777 W. BLUEMOUND RD. P.O. BOX 13819 MILWAUKEE, WI 53213

www.halleonard.com

1114